THE OFFICIAL
MANCHESTER UNITED
WWW.MANUTD.COM

ANNUAL
2002

Adam Bostock

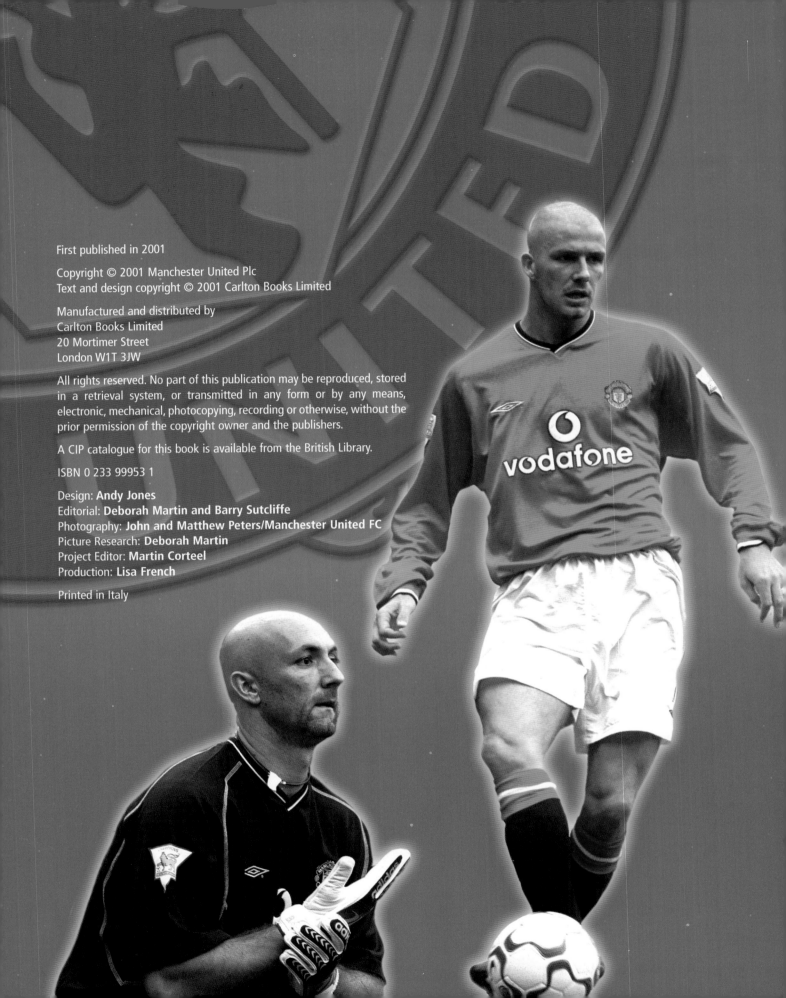

First published in 2001

Copyright © 2001 Manchester United Plc
Text and design copyright © 2001 Carlton Books Limited

Manufactured and distributed by
Carlton Books Limited
20 Mortimer Street
London W1T 3JW

A CIP catalogue for this book is available from the British Library.

ISBN 0 233 99953 1

Design: **Andy Jones**
Editorial: **Deborah Martin and Barry Sutcliffe**
Photography: **John and Matthew Peters/Manchester United FC**
Picture Research: **Deborah Martin**
Project Editor: **Martin Corteel**
Production: **Lisa French**

Printed in Italy

Contents

The Theatre of Dreams, Home of the Champions ... whichever way you describe it, the name of **Old Trafford** is recognised throughout the world as the place where 67,700 people go to watch top-quality live football. But where exactly is it, and what can you do there when the Reds aren't playing?

History

Manchester United first played at Old Trafford on 19 February 1910, when 50,000 people turned up to see them lose 4–3 to Liverpool. The club's president, John Henry Davies, had paid £60,000 for the plot of land on which the stadium was built.

When Matt Busby first took over as manager in 1945, the club couldn't play at Old Trafford because it had been badly damaged by bombs during the war. For a few seasons while it was being repaired, the Reds had to share the Maine Road ground of their rivals, Manchester City.

The road on which the stadium is situated is today named Sir Matt Busby Way. This name was adopted in 1994 after the death of United's great manager. A statue of Sir Matt now stands at the front of the ground, under the neon 'Manchester United' sign, looking out over the road towards the city.

can proudly show off all the silverware they have won. Hope the European Cup is in there when you next visit the Museum!

Location

United's stadium can be found in the Old Trafford district of Manchester, about two miles to the south-west of the city centre.

The nearest main-line railway station is Manchester Piccadilly, while the nearest tram (Metrolink) station is called Old Trafford and is next door to the world-famous cricket ground of the same name.

Old Trafford is approximately 168 miles to the north of the Millennium Stadium in Cardiff, where Ryan Giggs plays international football for Wales and where the FA Cup and Worthington Cup finals are held. United's ground is 209 miles south of Hampden Park in Glasgow, where the 2002 Champions League final will be played.

Museum
Tel. 0161 868 8631

The best place to find out more about the history of Manchester United is inside Old Trafford itself, at the club's museum. Located on Level 3 of the North Stand, the museum is one of North West England's most popular tourist attractions.

Obviously one of the most visited displays is the trophy cabinet, where United

Tour Centre
Tel. 0161 868 8631

Quite often the visitors to the Museum also book themselves on a special Stadium Tour. For this, an expert guide employed by Manchester United takes the fans inside the ground, but not on a match day when the players have work to do!

It takes about an hour to show the fans some of the inner corridors and secret places, such as the dressing room, the press lounge and the players' tunnel. You can even sit on the bench (like Ole Gunnar Solskjaer!) but nobody is allowed to walk on the pitch, by order of head groundsman, Keith Kent!

Trafford

Red Cafe
Tel. 0161 868 8303

Fans who feel a bit peckish after learning about the history in the Museum and taking in the sights of the Tour can always drop into Old Trafford's very own restaurant.

The Red Cafe isn't all about food and drink, though. There are television screens wherever you look, showing some classic action and goal clips from the Manchester United video archives.

Megastore
Tel. 0161 868 8567

One of the biggest football club shops in the world, the Megastore is easy to find but hard to escape from without buying anything!

The shop is crammed full of United gifts, souvenirs and replica kit – and like the Red Cafe, it has video screens and music to keep you entertained while you browse your way around.

The Megastore is on the ground floor of the East Stand.

Information

Main telephone number:
0161 868 8000

Postal address:
Manchester United FC, Sir Matt Busby Way, Old Trafford, Manchester M16 0RA.

Website address:
www.ManUtd.com
(contains lots of visitor info!)

2000/01 Season's Review

Re-rewind! When the crowd said **'goal'** on Sunday 20 August 2000, the Reds were up and running for their fifteenth season under Sir Alex Ferguson. It was to be another exciting campaign for United as they tried to win their third league title in a row, and to become the Champions of Europe once again. So did they manage it? Forgotten already? Then refresh your memory over the next ten action-packed pages…

August Action

After losing pre-season games to Bayern in Munich, and Chelsea in the Charity Shield, the Reds kicked off for real against Newcastle United. The streets around Old Trafford were buzzing for hours before the match as supporters piled into the Megastore to buy their new Vodafone-sponsored shirts. The away team, in their barcode-style black and white tops, went home empty-handed when Ronny Johnsen and Andrew Cole bagged two goals for the reigning Champions.

Two days later, on a Tuesday night, the Reds rolled down to Ipswich Town. It was like a party inside Portman Road as the Tractor Boys toasted their return to the Premiership, and the home fans had even more to cheer about when Fabian Wilnis scored the first Premiership goal against Fabien Barthez. David Beckham equalised with a curling free-kick, to make sure the entertaining contest finished in a draw.

Beckham did it again when the Reds arrived in East London for a tough match against West Ham. This time United took the lead with one of his fab free-kicks, then Cole craftily lofted the ball over Shaka Hislop for goal number two. The Reds were on a roll until the last six minutes when the Hammers hit back with a penalty by Paolo di Canio and Davor Suker's soft second goal. Bad defending made it a sad ending.

Hero: David Beckham was voted Player of the Month on ManUtd.com. More than 27,000 people voted, more than half of them said Becks was the best.

Villains: West Ham's Paolo di Canio and Davor Suker doubled up to steal two points from the Reds. It was daylight robbery!

Premiership position: 5th					
P:3	W:1	D:2	L:0	F:5	A:3

Points: 5
One behind the leaders, Arsenal

Left: Chelsea's Marcel Desailly (left) and referee Mike Riley usher Roy Keane to an early bath in the FA Charity Shield match.

Top: Barthez can't believe the outcome at Upton Park.

Superb September

For sixteen days, September looked superb. The Reds went on the rampage, blasting **Bradford** for six* and thumping three into the nets of **Sunderland** and **Everton**. Paul Scholes (2) and Teddy Sheringham won the battle of the England strikers at Old Trafford, scoring in United's 3–0 win while Sunderland's Kevin Phillips was foiled by the brilliance of Fabien Barthez. The French goalkeeper also pleased the crowd with his party-piece when he flicked the ball over the striker's head. Fan-tastique!

United were in great form at Goodison Park, where they made easy work of **Everton**. Nicky Butt knocked in the first goal, Ryan Giggs grabbed the second and Ole Gunnar Solskjaer struck the third, all before the break. Thomas Gravesen's goal was only a consolation, and the only blow was Barthez limping off.

Without Barthez and Jaap Stam, who'd been substituted in the **Sunderland** game, United's defence did not look its usual solid self in the last league game of September. The visiting team, **Chelsea**, took full advantage to take a point away from a thrilling 3–3 draw in which Scholes, Sheringham and Beckham all scored first-half goals.

Becks takes the applause of the away fans at Portman Road.

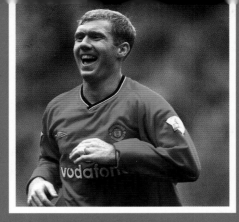

Hero: David Beckham – ManUtd.com's Player of the Month for the second month in a row.

Villain: Tore Andre Flo scored twice for Chelsea at Old Trafford, turning another win into a draw for United.

Premiership position: 1st					
P:7	W:4	D:3	L:0	F:20	A:7
Points: 15					
Level with Leicester City					

*For more details of this match, see our special feature on page 36, **Seven Deadly Wins!**

Above: **Scholes is all smiles after scoring against Sunderland at Old Trafford.**

Below: **Becks, Teddy and Ole celebrate an easy win at Everton.**

Top right: **Solskjaer's shot is too hot for Everton defender Steve Watson.**

Above: **Giggs goes for a run past Di Matteo (right) and Morris.**

Red October

The millions of fans who watched United and **Arsenal** go head-to-head must have gasped in awe when Thierry Henry scored a stupendous goal after 30 minutes. The Arsenal star knew he'd have to find something special to beat his French pal Fabien Barthez, and boy, did he find it! Arsenal's old boys, Tony Adams and Martin Keown, then played out of their skins to stop United scoring. So it was 1–0 to the Gunners in the game of the season, so far!

The Reds soon bounced back to knock **Leicester City** off the top spot in the table. Through team effort, the Champions patiently pieced together twenty-one passes to set up Teddy Sheringham's first-half header. Honest, we counted them all! Counting the goals was easier, though … it was Leicester 0 United 3.

If SuperTed didn't think his season could get any better, he was wrong! More was to come in the home match against **Southampton**,* and there was another great win at Old Trafford for the lads against **Leeds**.* Some of United's younger

players came out to play on Hallowe'en, at **Watford** in the Worthington Cup. The kids coped very well and won 3–0, thanks to their big brothers Ole (2) and Yorkie! Luke Chadwick had a top match, and even sub goalie Paul Rachubka did his bit, after Rai van der Gouw was sent off.

Top left: **'SuperTed' heads United into the lead at Leicester City.**

Right – top/bottom: **Ole goes for goal against Watford … and scores!**

Hero: Teddy Sheringham – he scored a hat-trick, and was voted Player of the Month on ManUtd.com.

Villain: Thierry Henry, but it was still a top goal by the Gunner. This rival deserves respect!

Premiership position: 1st					
P:11	W:7	D:3	L:1	F:31	A:8
Points: **24**. Level on points with Arsenal.					

Nearly perfect November

So-called because the Reds nearly won all of their matches in the month! Losing 2–1 at Sunderland in the Worthington Cup was the only blip, but it was still some battle with the game going into extra-time after Reds scorer Yorkie was shown the red card.

United started the month on a high note at Highfield Road by racing into the lead against **Coventry** with a lightning move finished off by Andrew Cole, and a free-kick blasted through the wall by Becks. The Sky Blues tried to catch up, but could only score one against Fabien.

Luke Chadwick makes his first Premiership start against Derby County at Pride Park.

Becks takes care of the local business – City 0, United 1.

Middlesbrough briefly dreamed of a surprise victory when dreadlocked star Christian Karembeu gave them the lead. But two goals in three minutes by Butt and Sheringham soon brought them back down to earth! The crowd roared United on to beat Boro, and there was also a great atmosphere inside **Manchester City's** Maine Road ground when the Reds beat the Blues in the local derby. All it took was one free-kick from David Beckham in the first half – and wham! The kings of England were still the kings of Manchester.

From the local derby to **Derby County**, United were still in the winning mood when they raided the Rams for three more goals and three more points. Sheringham, Yorke and Butt did us proud at Pride Park.

Hero: Teddy Sheringham – top man of the month once again for ManUtd.com. More than half of the votes went to SuperTed for scoring yet more important goals.

Villain: Mr Halsey, the match official who sent off Yorkie at **Sunderland**. Leave it out, ref!

Premiership position: 1st					
P:15	W:11	D:3	L:1	F:39	A:10
Points: **36**. The Reds were still top at the end of November, and 8 points clear of Arsenal.					

*For more details of this match, see our special feature on page 36, **Seven Deadly Wins!**

Dynamic December

The best match in December was a real ding-donger, away from home, which the Reds didn't win! Instead, they shared six goals with cheeky **Charlton**, who came back from 3–1 down to draw 3–3. Giggsy had a great game, hitting the bar from the half-way line. Almost a Christmas cracker!

Beckham and Giggs join Keane to celebrate his goal against Charlton at The Valley .

Solskjaer shows Ipswich Town just what he thinks of 'em!

There were more points when **Spurs** and **Ipswich** both took the long road home after losing 2–0. Trust Liverpool, though, to ruin United's festive fun by beating them 1–0. That hurt!

On Boxing Day, the Reds sneaked a win down at **Aston Villa** when on-form Ole scored the only goal. Then it was back up north, to nippy **Newcastle** where the teams drew 1–1. So the year 2000 ended with the Reds still standing tall on top. But would it be a happy New Year?

Hero: Ole Gunnar Solskjaer. The super-sub proved he can also score goals when he starts matches!

Villain: Danny Murphy. The Liverpool midfielder had the nerve to score a free-kick, Becks-style!

Premiership position: 1st					
P:21	W:14	D:5	L:2	F:48	A:15

Points: **47.** United were top at the end of December, still 8 points clear of Arsenal.

Joyful January

After a triumphant Christmas, the United faithful were treated to a joyful January, during which the Reds won five of their six matches. It all started on New Year's Day with a real hammering of **West Ham*** at Old Trafford, and the month ended with a battling victory away at **Sunderland.***

In between, the Champions had to play two home matches, and two back-to-back away games against the clubs who were expected to change places at the end of the season – Fulham and Bradford City.

First Division high-flyers **Fulham** showed no fear in the FA Cup tie, especially when Fabrice Fernandez broke through the United ranks to equalise. Missing Barthez, Stam and Scholes, United needed to bring on Teddy Sheringham to win the tie 2–1.

The Premiership's bottom club, **Bradford,** had a bad day when Teddy Sheringham scored the simplest of tap-ins, after ex-United keeper Gary Walsh had completely missed the ball with his clumsy boot! It was a great day for Ryan Giggs though, who fired in another cracker, and for Luke Chadwick, who scored his first-ever goal for United.

Later, back at Old Trafford, there was a straightforward 2–0 win over **Aston Villa.** Gary Neville will tell you it was a special game, but only because he scored for a change!

*For more details of these matches, see our special feature on page 36, **Seven Deadly Wins!**

Sadly not even goal machine Gary could score in the next home game, to save United's FA Cup campaign. **West Ham's** Di Canio did find the net, though, beating Barthez who bizarrely tried to psyche him out by standing still with his arm in the air. These world-class keepers are crazy!

Hero: Ryan Giggs. Back to his dazzling best, winning the Player of the Month poll on ManUtd.com.

Villain: Paolo Di Canio, for scoring against United for the second time in the season, and knocking them out of the Cup.

Premiership position: 1st					
P:25	W:18	D:5	L:2	F:57	A:16

Points: **59.** The Reds were 15 points clear of second-placed Arsenal at the end of January.

Goal machine Gary Neville (left) shares a joke with his team mates.

Yorke (left) and Solskjaer in party mood
on New Year's Day.

Funny Old February

Funny because United bagged more goals in one half against **Arsenal**, than they did in all of their other February games put together!

Until the Dwight Yorke show took over against the Gunners, the Reds really struggled to score. They needed Steve Watson's own-goal to beat **Everton**, while Andrew Cole was the only man to find a way past **Chelsea**'s defence in the 1–1 draw at Stamford Bridge.

Maybe United's own defence should take some of the credit for a change. Jaap Stam and Wes Brown formed a big barrier at the back, while Roy Keane ran the length and breadth of the park in another important, unbeaten month.

Hero: Roy Keane played like a true captain through a difficult month and pipped Wes and Yorkie to the Player of the Month award.

Villain: Chelsea's Jimmy Floyd Hasselbaink, who scored against the Reds for the second time in 2000/01.

Right: **The hat-trick hero celebrates.**
Below: **Reds paying their respects to Dwight.**

Keane on a mission to maul Arsenal.

Premiership position: 1st					
P:28	W:20	D:6	L:2	F:65	A:18

Points: 66. United were 16 points ahead of Arsenal at the end of February.

Marching On

From one big match to another, United followed their thrashing of **Arsenal** with a tricky trip to **Leeds**, who were starting to make waves in the Champions League.

Somehow the Reds stayed afloat in a stormy match at Elland Road, thanks to Fabien Barthez saving Ian Harte's penalty just before half-time and to Luke Chadwick's opening goal. Luckily, too, the linesman cancelled out worried Wes Brown's last minute own-goal. If Brown's blunder had counted, Leeds would have won the match 2–1, having only just equalised with Mark Viduka's powerful header. Phew!

Fantastic Fabien unfortunately missed the next league match, at home to **Leicester**. He didn't miss much though, as the shy old Foxes hardly crossed the half-way line. No problems then for Paul Rachubka, who kept a clean sheet on his Premiership debut, but frustrating for United fans who had to wait until very late in the day for subs Silvestre and Yorkie to score for a 2–0 win.

Sadly there was no happy ending to the month of March as United lost 2–0 at **Liverpool**. It was a poor performance and a poor result, but at least the Reds still had a big lead to cushion the blow.

Hero: Fabien Barthez. Missed a game, but saved a penalty.

Villain: Robbie Fowler. The Liverpool lad has a knack of scoring against United.

Premiership position: 1st					
P:31	W:21	D:7	L:3	F:68	A:21

Points: 70. United's lead had been cut down to a mere 13 points by the end of March!

Below: **Luke scores at Leeds and** (main picture) **celebrates with Becks and Teddy.**
Below left: **Happy days for Chadwick (left) and Butt.**

April Ecstasy

The disappointment of losing at **Liverpool** and then at home to **Bayern Munich** (see the Champions League feature on page 32) made the Reds all the more determined to wrap up the Premiership title. First in the firing line were **Charlton Athletic** – and, boy, did they know about it! United hit the target eight times, but somehow only scored twice, through Andrew Cole in the first-half, and Ole Gunnar Solskjaer very late in the second half. Still, that was enough to beat the Addicks 2–1 at Old Trafford on a Tuesday night.

That result meant the title could be clinched just four days later on Easter Saturday. Nobody quite expected it to happen, but it did, thanks to United's exciting 4–2 win over **Coventry City*** and Arsenal's very surprising 3–0 defeat at home to Middlesbrough. That was that, the Reds were Champions again!

With the title already won, and **Manchester City** already looking doomed, the second derby match of the season lacked a bit of spark. Until, that is, the last half-hour when Scholes missed a penalty, Sheringham scored one, Steve Howey equalised for 1–1 and Roy Keane was sent off for clattering Alf-Inge Haaland.

Silvestre sets off on a flying run against Charlton Athletic.

The next match, at **Middlesbrough**, started like the City game ended … explosively! Luckily this time it was talent rather than temper which took everyone by surprise, when Phil Neville knocked in one of the goals of the season by firing into the top corner in the fourth minute. David Beckham also did his bit, blasting in his ninth goal of the season to make the final score 2–0 to the Reds in dark blue shirts.

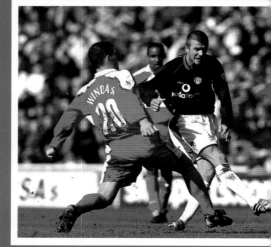

Beckham (in blue) rattles in goal number two at Boro.

Hero: Fabien Barthez caught 31 per cent of the Player of the Month votes on ManUtd.com.

Villains: Steve Howey scored the late equaliser for City in the Manchester derby.

Sheringham snatches the ball from Charlton Athletic.

Premiership position: Champs					
P:35	W:24	D:8	L:3	F:77	A:25

Points: 80. The Reds were 14 points ahead of Arsenal at the end of April, with only 12 points left to play for!

Head down, leg straight – textbook stuff from Cole at Tottenham.

Silvestre sorts out the Spurs.

May Parade

Party-time! After bottling up their emotions for two games, the Reds could finally spray the champagne around on 5 May 2001 and celebrate their seventh Premiership title in nine seasons. Losing 1–0 to **Derby County** didn't seem to matter, the fans at Old Trafford really just wanted to see the silverware after the final home match had ended. The fireworks and flags, scarves and soldiers made it a special scene for the lucky United supporters who saw the trophy and medals handed over to their heroes.

But the season didn't end there, of course. No more league points were needed, but some of the young players selected by Sir Alex Ferguson had personal points to prove. Michael Stewart, Ronnie Wallwork and Luke Chadwick all started in the 2–1 defeat at The Dell, United's last-ever match at the **Southampton** ground. And although some of the stars returned when the Reds lost 3–1 to **Tottenham Hotspur** at White Hart Lane, there was still room for Bojan Djordjic to make his debut, coming on as sub to play the final 13 minutes of the season.

It wasn't the way United would have wished to end the campaign, with three defeats in a row, but at least the Championship trophy was staying put … proudly in place at the Old Trafford museum!

Hero: Sir Alex Ferguson, the first manager in England to win three Championships in a row.

Villain: Willem Korsten struck twice for Spurs to make it three defeats in a row for the Champions.

Premiership position: Champs					
P38	W:24	D:8	L:6	F:79	A:31

Points: 80. The Champions finished the season with 10 points more than the runners-up, Arsenal.

*For more details of this match, see our special feature on page 36, **Seven Deadly Wins!**

Southampton's Kachloul can't catch Chadwick (in blue).

Bald

is beautiful

They used to say the first sight of Wembley's Twin Towers tested the nerve of England's top footballers. But now some of the country's best strikers bottle it when they see the shiny domes in United's defence …

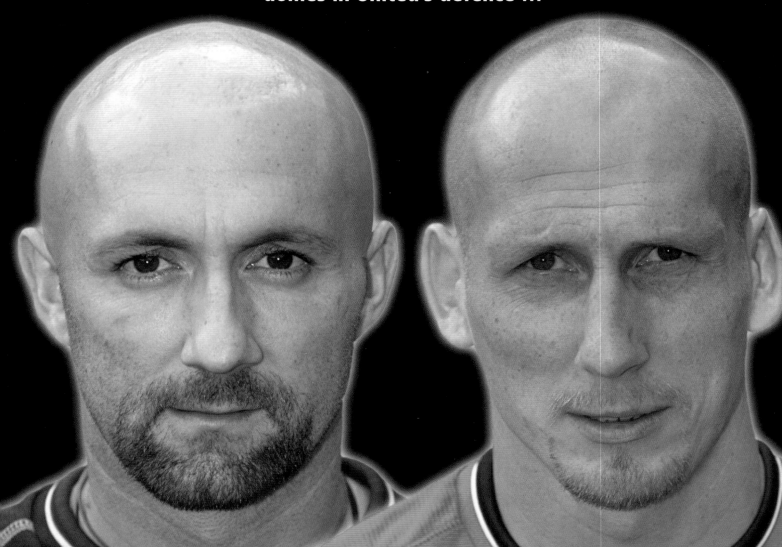

FABIEN BARTHEZ

2000/01 record:
43 games, 0 goals

If you somehow manage to beat the United defence, you've still got to beat this man. That was the daunting prospect for teams in the Premiership and Champions League, who had been hoping and praying that Peter Schmeichel's departure would weaken the Reds. Maybe it did for a while, but then along came Fabien Barthez, signed from Monaco.

Barthez is simply the best in the world in his position … and that's official! Not only because he plays in goal for the World and European champions, France, but also because the International Federation of Football History & Statistics voted him the best keeper on the planet. No wonder opposition forwards don't fancy their chances of scoring when they face Fabien!

During his first season with United, Fabien produced some outstanding performances, especially those against Panathinaikos in Athens, Bayern Munich at Old Trafford, and Leeds at Elland Road, where he saved Ian Harte's penalty. No team scored more than two goals past him in a single game.

Fabien's success is based on his agility, strength, stamina, speed and his ability to pluck crosses out of the air as if they were apples on a tree. So it's just an added bonus that he can play with his feet as well! Perhaps his favourite trick is where he tempts an opponent to rush forward, and then proceeds to either dribble the ball around him, flick it

over his head or nutmeg him! It might look crazy, and sometimes he comes very close to being caught, but Fabien loves to entertain the United fans.

It's still early days in the love affair between Fabien Barthez and Manchester United, but from what we've seen so far, it could turn out to be a real epic. There's much, much more to come from the mad Frenchman!

Did you know? Fabien's transfer fee from Monaco to Manchester United, £7.8 million, was a British record for a goalkeeper.

JAAP STAM

2000/01 record:
22 games, 0 goals

The player described by Sir Alex Ferguson as the best man-marker in Europe is used to winning his battles on the field, no matter who the opposing striker is. But even Jaap Stam had to surrender during 2000/01 when he finally decided to have an operation on his injured ankle, and missed four months of action.

Believe it or not, the big Dutchman had carried the injury, on and off, through the previous season. But so great were his performances in 1999/2000 that nobody spotted the problem, except for the attentive and secretive United physios.

Jaap is the sort of man who can play through the pain barrier, as he proved in Euro 2000 when television cameras showed a close-up of him having stitches in his head during a match for Holland against Czechoslovakia. The only thing the physios couldn't fix was his wounded pride, after his sky-high penalty miss sent the Orange Army tumbling out of the tournament they were expected to win!

After sitting out through September, October, November and December 2000, Jaap returned to the United team in January 2001 and – surprise, surprise – in his first seven matches back in the side, they kept five clean sheets! Perhaps his best performance was in the cauldron of the Mestalla Stadium, where he stifled the Valencia strikers and in turn their supporters, in the 0–0 draw that was a real defensive masterclass.

Yet there is something still missing from Stam's game – goals! The United fans raise the volume whenever Jaap goes on one of his surging runs forward, but in three years he's not found the net at Old Trafford. Not even from one of the many situations when David Beckham beams the ball to his bonce from the corner flag!

Stam's goal tally was still stuck on one, at the end of 2000/2001. Mind you, there's plenty of time for him to increase it – Jaap signed a new contract with United in 2001 and hopes to stay with the Reds until the end of his top-class career.

Did you know? Jaap started his career with a small Dutch club called PEC Zwolle.

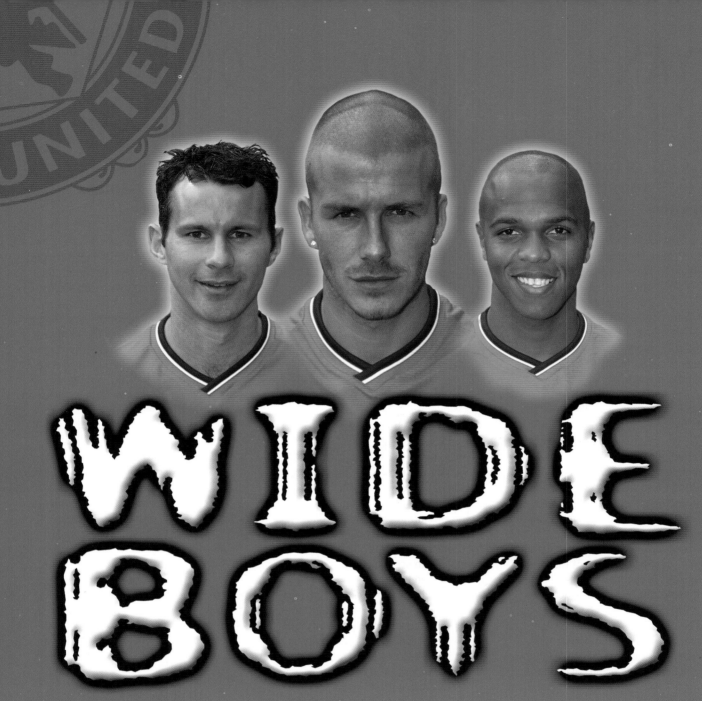

WIDE BOYS

Top-class strikers like **Andrew Cole** and **Ruud van Nistelrooy** need first-class service, so they'll thank their lucky stars that **Manchester United** have two of the best wingers in the world, plus a rising star from South Africa …

RYAN GIGGS

2000/01 record:
35 (+ 9 subs) games, 7 goals

Ryan has been running rings around defenders for over ten years, but if players peak when they're 29 or 30, there's still much more to come from the Cardiff kid! The Welsh wizard would like nothing more than to mark his testimonial season, 2001/02, by winning some more silverware for Sir Alex Ferguson. Another Treble would be the perfect leaving present from Ryan to the boss who made him into a superstar, after calling at his home on his 14th birthday and asking him to sign for United.

Ryan will always be remembered for goals like the amazing one which knocked Arsenal out of the FA Cup in 1999, and he produced more moments of magic during 2000/01. His personal goal of the season was against Bradford, when he dribbled down the left to score with a deadly diagonal strike. Against Charlton, he came close to copying Beckham, when he hit the crossbar with a shot from the half-way line!

Ryan's remarkable range of skills also includes accurate heading, as demonstrated on Easter Saturday 2001 when he nodded the ball up and over the Coventry goalkeeper to give United the lead on the day they clinched the Championship. It wasn't his last goal of the season, but it was certainly the most important. The next one he scored was sadly in vain, as United lost 2–1 to Bayern Munich in the European Cup. It was a disappointing night for the Reds, but with Ryan still around, they're sure to bounce back, big style!

Did you know? Ryan's current contract, signed during the 2000/01 season, should keep him at United until 2006!

DAVID BECKHAM

2000/01 record:
42 (+ 3 subs) games, 9 goals

Believe it or not, David's favourite position isn't out on the wing, where he can smell the touchline paint and hear even the whispers in the crowd. But while he's still delivering deadly crosses for Cole and co. to convert into goals, there seems little chance that Becks will ever play where he really wants to – in the centre of midfield. Sir Alex Ferguson wants him to stay on the right wing, and to stay with the club for good. You won't hear David moaning about that – he's just delighted to be playing for the team he supported as a boy.

In 2000/01, David again played an important part in winning the title, right from the word go! He obviously had Sir Alex Ferguson's words ringing in his ears, asking him to score more goals, because Becks blasted home in three games on the bounce as the season kicked in, against Ipswich Town, West Ham and Bradford City. He later scored with two more of those special free-kicks, away to Coventry, and at Maine Road where his goal settled the Manchester derby 1–0 in United's favour.

David also enjoyed some great moments as an England player in 2000/01, when he made another of his boyhood dreams come true by captaining his country. Later in the season, he scored a crucial goal against Finland at Anfield. That was a strange afternoon for David, being cheered at a ground where he's normally jeered. But even the Liverpool fans know how important he is to England, no matter which club he plays for!

Did you know? David was voted second best player in Europe and the World in 2000. Rivaldo was voted best in both cases.

QUINTON FORTUNE

2000/01 record:
8 (+ 2 subs) games, 2 goals

Quinton Fortune needs more than luck and skill to make his name in football, and he also needs patience while he competes for a first team place with Beckham and Giggs. Their world-class form kept Quinton out of the picture during 2000/01, but he was also out of the country for a while, when he played for South Africa at the Sydney Olympics. The trip was badly timed – he flew to Australia just after bagging two goals for the Reds against Bradford – but it was still a great experience, especially when he scored against Brazil!

Did you know? Manchester United won the FA Cup, beating Liverpool 2–1, on the same day in 1977 that Quinton was born. Talk about good fortune!

If Sir Alex Ferguson had a pound for every rumour that was ever written about Manchester United in the newspapers, he could probably pay for Ronaldo, Rivaldo and Ruud van Nistelrooy out of his own pocket! But thankfully not everything you read or hear about the Reds is just a fairytale. In fact, the manager, players and officials are always telling true stories to the club's own media …

READ ALL

PROGRAMME

In the good old days, long before digital television and text messages, the match programme was the only source of information about the club which the club produced itself. The programme sold on every match day at Old Trafford is called the United Review and contains team news, articles about the opposition, fixtures, results and news from around the ground.

MAGAZINES

The *United Review* stood alone until December 1992 when the official Manchester United magazine was first published. Bigger than a programme and sold in shops around the country, this

glossy monthly publication soon became very popular with the fans for its in-depth player interviews and exclusive photographs. After all, where else might you see a picture of Ryan Giggs in the kitchen or of Alex Ferguson playing snooker? A second magazine called *Glory Glory Man United* was later introduced for young fans, and features lots of player posters and special competitions.

RADIO

One of the best ways to follow a football match, if you haven't got a ticket, is to listen to live commentary on the radio. So launching its own radio station seemed the natural thing for the club to do in March 1994. Like the *United Review,* Manchester

ABOUT 'EM!

United Radio is only available on the day of a home match at Old Trafford. It broadcasts to the local area on 1413 medium wave from a few hours before kick-off, day or night, until a couple of hours after the final whistle. Tune in next time you're there!

INTERNET

Easily the best way to follow a match if you're far, far away is through the club's official website, www.ManUtd.com. This first hit the Internet in August 1998, perfectly timed to cover the Treble-winning season with daily news stories and match reports published during and after the big games. From his seat in the stadium, the webmaster can send details of every throw-in, free-kick, corner, shot and goal to thousands of computers around the world.

MOBILE PHONES

Manchester United's webmaster also feeds news and match information to fans who are on the move, via text messages to mobile phones. This manUmobile service has been created with the help of Vodafone, the club's shirt sponsors, and is a real bonus for supporters who have to go shopping on a Saturday afternoon when they'd rather be following the match on the PC or the radio!

TELEVISION

The world's first daily television channel to be devoted to one football club proudly went on air for the first time in September 1998. Again, it was great timing, as the cameras followed the team on their travels to the glorious Treble, in England and abroad. Fully approved by the players and most important, by Sir Alex Ferguson himself, MUTV broadcasts match coverage, classic action, news, interviews, quiz programmes, talk shows and footage from behind the scenes. It's on air every evening, on satellite and cable television.

BOOKS

Another place where you can read all about the Reds is in the bookshop. Every year, a range of new Manchester United books appears on the shelves, with something to interest fans of all ages. Stats and facts lovers can dive into the official encyclopedia, illustrated history and the yearbook. Meanwhile, any fans looking for fun and games can browse through books of quizzes, quotes and activities. It's the perfect way to pass all that boring time between matches!

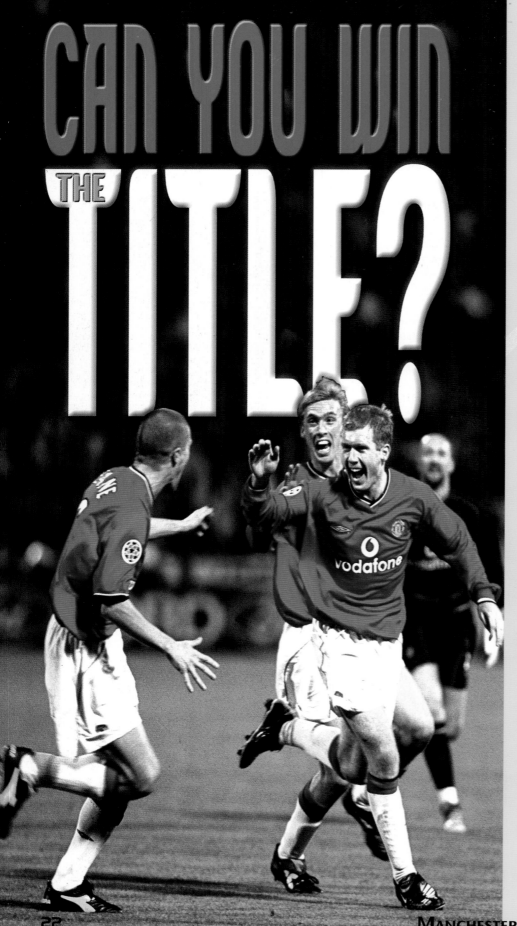

CAN YOU WIN THE TITLE?

Welcome to the **biggest** quiz in the book! There are no prizes at stake, only points and pride as you try to match Sir Alex Ferguson by winning the title ...

The FA Carling Premiership is still **the hardest competition.** It's no good being a flash in the pan, or lucky on the day; you have to last the pace and perform well through 38 matches. Or in this case, 38 questions! Your only opponent is the clock, so you might want a friend or relative to act as time-keeper and referee.

Please note: All questions regarding goals, games and results are based on the 2000/01 season.

Scoring: 3 points for every correct answer from memory; 1 point for a correct answer if you have to leaf through the book to find it; 0 points if you get the answer wrong, or fail to answer within the time limit. When you've worked through all 38 questions, calculate your points total and then measure it against our league ranking system, to see if you're doomed for the drop, stuck in mid-table or up for the title!

Time limit: 30 seconds to answer each question. Be quick!

1 Who collected two Player of the Year awards before the opening Premiership match?

2 Who had a black eye when the team photograph was taken in August 2000?

3 Against which club did Quinton Fortune score two goals in September?

4 Who described Paul Scholes as the 'only English player with world-class technical ability'?

5 What is the job title of United's main man in a suit, Peter Kenyon?

6 On which ground did United claim their first away win in the Premiership?

7 What is the name of Vodafone's special information service for United fans?

8 What is Sir Alex Ferguson's middle name?

9 What is the name of United's goalkeeping coach?

10 Who scored United's first Premiership goal of the season?

11 Who is the head groundsman at Manchester United Football Club?

12 Which young player used to play for Arsenal Schoolboys?

13 Who was sent off in the FA Charity Shield match against Chelsea?

14 What is the name of the official Manchester United movie?

15 Which two United players were sent off in the Worthington Cup?

16 Who scored the opening goal for Middlesbrough at Old Trafford?

17 What was the half-time score in the Manchester derby at Maine Road?

18 What was the half-time score when United thrashed Arsenal at Old Trafford?

19 Who celebrated his 35th birthday and scored a penalty in the month of April 2001?

20 Who were United playing when Wes Brown scored an own goal in the Champions League?

21 Which team was the first to prevent United from scoring in a Premiership match?

22 Which two teams, beginning with the same letter, did United draw 3–3 with?

23 Which opposition team is sometimes known as the Tractor Boys?

24 What was spooky about the night when United played at Watford?

25 Which country did United visit last in the 2000/01 Champions League?

26 On which special day of the year does Sir Alex Ferguson celebrate his birthday?

27 What is the address of United's official website?

28 What is the name of the club's doctor?

29 Against which Premiership club did Teddy Sheringham score a hat-trick?

30 What was the name of the referee who sent off Dwight Yorke at Sunderland?

31 Which Chelsea player scored both home and away against United?

32 Which two United players sat among the fans when the team won 3–0 at Leicester City?

33 Which United player took part in the 2000 Olympics in Sydney?

34 Whose penalty did Fabien Barthez save at Leeds?

35 Which two teams, beginning with the same letter, did United score four goals against in April?

36 Which team beat Arsenal to clinch the title for United on Easter Saturday?

37 On which ground did United end their Premiership season?

38 How much did the Reds pay for Ruud Van Nistelrooy in Dutch money?

Check your answers on page 60.

RATINGS

If you scored between **0 and 35 points,** oh dear! Your poor memory and lack of knowledge mean you can only go in one direction, down to Division One. Sack the manager!

If you scored between **36 and 45 points,** you've survived in the Premiership by the skin of your teeth! Must try harder next season, or else the Chairman will get very restless.

An average score of **46 to 54 points** would make you an average manager. The fans are not over-excited by your performance, but there's no cause for concern. Just the boredom of finishing in mid-table.

A respectable score of **55 to 60 points** would give you the chance to enter European competitions, by the back door! You'll have to cut short your summer holiday and play in the Inter-Toto Cup.

If your score was **61 to 70 points**, you can celebrate finishing fourth or fifth in the Premiership and claiming a guaranteed place in the UEFA Cup. Next season could be even better!

A score of **71 to 80 points** is excellent and worthy of a place in the Champions League. Well done! The only disappointment is that you weren't quite good enough to win the title. Better luck next time.

If you score more than **80 points**, CONGRATULATIONS! You've won the title! Go on, treat yourself to a glass of champagne or, if you're under 18, a can of cola! All you have to do now is win the Champions League.

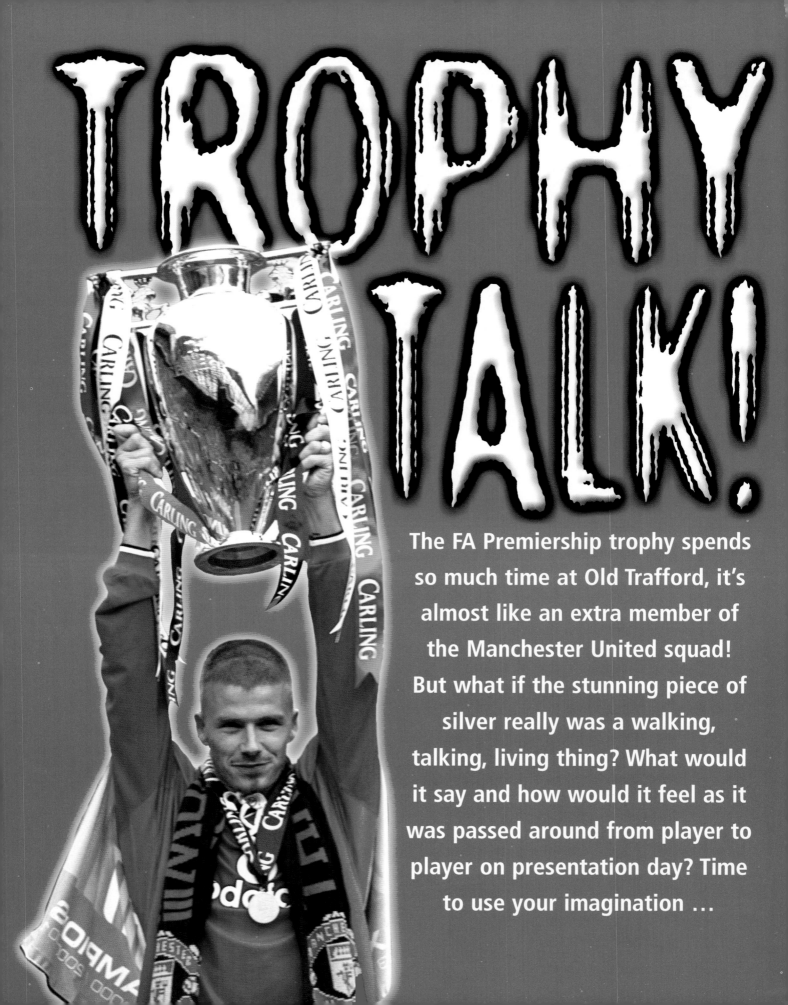

TROPHY TALK!

The FA Premiership trophy spends so much time at Old Trafford, it's almost like an extra member of the Manchester United squad! But what if the stunning piece of silver really was a walking, talking, living thing? What would it say and how would it feel as it was passed around from player to player on presentation day? Time to use your imagination …

"Here's a familiar scene. There's me, look, in the middle, surrounded by some of my favourite players. Coley, Ryan, Gary, Keano … I've known them all for years."

"Here I am inside the dressing room. I couldn't understand a word these two were saying to each other. I think they were speaking in Norse code!"

"I hadn't met this Fabien guy before, but he was a top geezer with an amazing grip. I always felt safe in his hands – I just knew he wouldn't drop me! But, hey, where's my crown?"

"The man holding me in this photo, Sir Alex Ferguson, has only let me leave Old Trafford twice. After the last time, in 1998, he promised it wouldn't happen again!"

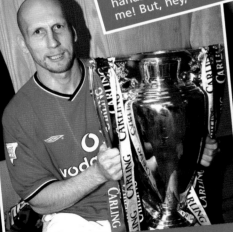

"Mr Stam from Holland is one of my favourite players. I think his first name's Edam, at least that's what he said when the photographer asked him to say 'Cheese'!"

"What a couple of snazzy dressers! Andrew and Dwight looked the business, but then so did I, dressed in my party-gear of red, white and black ribbons. Hope I'll be wearing the same again next year …"

"There's Sir Alex again, taking his turn on the mike. Don't worry, though, he didn't sing!"

CORNERSTONES

Most full-backs in football are like the rook pieces in chess. Steady, reliable, their success is in keeping the game simple. But when you're a full-back for Manchester United, you have to do a little bit more than just defend and pass. Sometimes you have to score goals yourself …

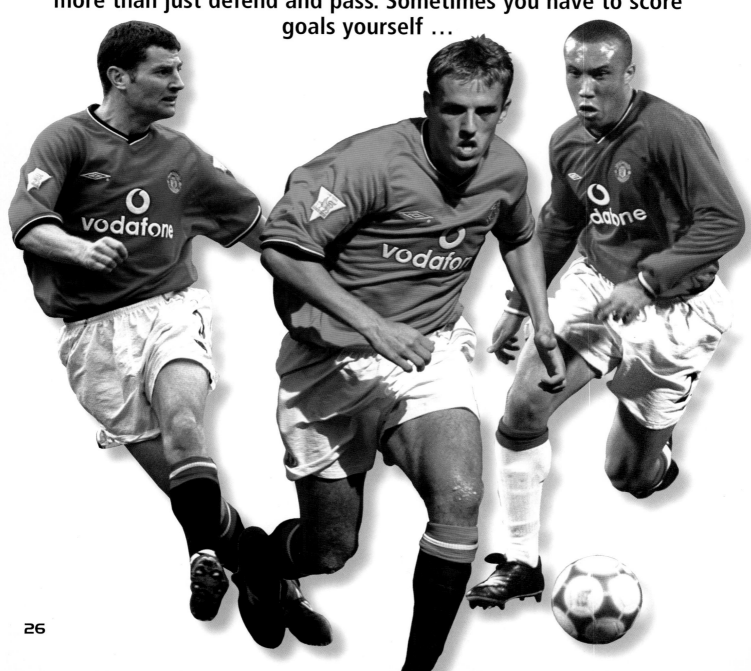

DENIS IRWIN

2000/01 record:
25 (+ 1 sub) games,
2 goals

Denis Irwin had to make a big decision about his future at the end of 2000/01, after losing his regular place in the team to younger men like Mikael Silvestre and Phil Neville.

It was ironic for Irwin that he was injured in his own testimonial match before the season even started. Not any old pre-season friendly, it was instead a very physical derby match against Manchester City, which the Reds won 2–0.

In his first game back, Denis bagged United's 200th goal in the European Cup/Champions League with a penalty in the 5–1 home win over Anderlecht. He doubled his tally for the season when he scored another spot-kick against the same opponents in Belgium.

He also helped to set up goals for other players, including two for Teddy Sheringham at Leicester City. Those forward runs at Filbert Street proved he was still fit enough for top-class football but for how long will he prove it with United?

Did you know? Denis Irwin beat his Old Trafford team-mates, including Ryan Giggs in the final, to win a special penalty competition organised by *Glory, Glory Man United* magazine in 2001.

PHIL NEVILLE

2000/01 record:
28 (+ 7 sub) games,
1 goal

When Phil Neville scored with a magnificent shot to give United the lead at Middlesbrough, he actually netted an equaliser for himself in the personal battle to score as many goals as his brother. Phil had been trailing for several months of the season, after Gary grabbed his rare moment of glory against Aston Villa!

The Nevilles, of course, are not known for their shooting boots, and their record for not scoring is something of a standing joke in the United dressing room. Phil even has a funny nickname, Jigsaw, because he apparently goes to pieces in the box. Maybe that's why he blasted the goal at Boro from long range …?

The great thing for Phil is that he can laugh along with the jokers, because he knows he's still part of a winning team – whether he scores or not. After all, Manchester United mainly employ him to do what he does best, defend. He's been doing that very well, thank you, ever since he captained the junior team to FA Youth Cup glory in 1995.

True, there are some moments he'd rather forget, like giving away penalties to Arsenal in 1999 (Bergkamp missed anyway) and Romania in Euro 2000 (they scored), but all the best defenders have to learn from their mistakes. Phil Neville is still learning, but he's already one of the best full-backs in England.

Did you know? Phil was sporting a black eye when the official team photograph for 2000/01 was taken. Ouch!

MIKAEL SILVESTRE

2000/01 record:
39 (+ 5 sub) games, 1 goal

There are very few defenders in football who look better on the break than Mikael Silvestre. The fleet-footed Frenchman raced forward many times during 2000/01, including the game against Leicester City when he came on as sub and scored his first goal for the club.

For that exciting part of his game, playing at full-back suits Silvestre very well. He still prefers to be in the centre of defence, just like he was in his first season at United, but he knows that playing on the left-hand side will allow him to link up with Ryan Giggs and join the attack more often.

You get the feeling there are more goals to come for Manchester United from mild-mannered Mik. He's already scored one for France, after breaking into the world's greatest national team in February 2001. In fact, it was quite a special year for the young star, as he also became a father for the first time and then won his second Premiership title with the Reds!

Did you know? Mikael's pet dog is named after one of his favourite cartoon characters, Homer Simpson.

HEARTBEAT

All the best teams need hard heads and brave hearts at the centre of their defence, and Manchester United are no exception. Alongside the world's greatest central defender, Jaap Stam, the Reds can pick from two of England's finest and an ice-cool Norwegian …

GARY NEVILLE RONNY JOHNSEN WES BROWN

2000/01 record:
48 games, 1 goal

2000/01 record:
14 games, 1 goal

2000/01 record:
36 (+ 5 sub) games, 0 goals

You might think this is a game of spot the deliberate mistake. But while many still think of Gary Neville as a hard-working right-back who does a sterling job for club and country, there are others who rate him very highly at the heart of United's defence.

During the 2000/01 title-winning season, Gaz filled in for Jaap Stam to form a great centre-back partnership with Ronny Johnsen and then Wes Brown. But even when the big Dutchman returned, the elder Neville didn't step out straightaway – they played some matches together in the middle. Gary even scored in one game, against Aston Villa at Old Trafford, to keep up his career average of about one goal per every one hundred appearances!

The England defender's next ambition will be to score an international goal, in the right net … in 2001, he unluckily scored an own-goal for Finland when a ball bounced off his leg past David Seaman at Anfield. Fortunately Gary set up Michael Owen's equaliser, then David Beckham made the final score 2–1 to England.

Did you know? Gary sat with David Beckham amongst the United fans when they didn't play in the match at Leicester City in 2001.

While Wes Brown largely steered clear of Carrington's casualty ward in 2000/01, Ronny Johnsen was again a regular patient there, after picking up another knee injury. It was a terrible twist of fate for the Norwegian international, who only played three games in the season before – including the one in which the Championship was finally won, at Southampton!

Ronny's hopes of playing a bigger part in the next triumph were boosted when he scored the very first goal of the 2000/01 campaign, at home to Newcastle, and he started eleven of the first fifteen games. But soon after, the bad luck struck, and after facing Sunderland in the Worthington Cup, he didn't play again until April 28. By then, the title had already been won, but Ronny then reminded Reds fans of his pace and power when he played out the remaining Premiership games.

Did you know? Ronny was nicknamed the 'Miracle of Marseille' after his blinding performance for Norway against Brazil in France '98. He practically marked Ronaldo out of the game!

Wesley Brown came bouncing back in 2000/01, after missing all of the previous season with a serious knee injury. It was a cruel blow for the promising young defender, having to sit on the sidelines at the time when his career should have been rocketing to greater heights. But Wes showed that time can be a great healer, and after patiently working away to regain his fitness, he returned to action at Everton in September 2000. The Reds were missing Stam and Johnsen that day, but Neville and Brown were brilliant.

One of Brown's best spells in the side was in October and November 2000, when the team conceded only three goals in the eight games he started in a row. Many opposition forwards then, and later in the season, were foiled by Wesley's speed, his ability in the air and his grace under pressure. Sir Alex Ferguson simply described him as 'the best natural defender this club has had for years and years'.

Give it time and Wes will soon be playing on the biggest stage of them all, at the World Cup Finals. Who knows, he might even captain his country one day, like his United team-mate David Beckham.

Did you know? The United fans sing about Wes to the tune of a popular old song called 'Knees Up, Mother Brown'. Altogether now … 'We've got Wesley Brown, we've got Wesley Brown …'

Engine Room

Every title-winning machine needs a red-hot engine room. So it's just as well that United have three great players to stoke the fires of the team, even when there's sometimes only room for two…

NICKY BUTT

2000/01 record:
34 (+ 7 sub) games, 4 goals

The tigerish midfielder from Gorton in Manchester gave the manager his favourite kind of problem in the 2000/01 season … who to leave out?! So good were Nicky's performances that he could no longer be seen as a spare part, the third member of a two-man central midfield.

Sir Alex Ferguson just couldn't leave him out, so at times he played all three of his aces … Keane, Scholes and Butt all together in the same team. A few times that meant a rest for Ryan Giggs. Nearly always it spelled trouble for the opposition who couldn't get a moment's peace in possession without Butt or one of his fellow ball-winners breaking up the play.

When he has the ball himself, Nicky can be dangerous, as he proved with goals against Everton, Middlesbrough, Sturm Graz and Derby County. Sturm, especially, felt the full force of his powerplay. First he struck a venomous goal low into the net from 25 yards, and then he tackled one of the Austrian players to gear up Teddy Sheringham for a goal. And all this inside the first twenty minutes!

Did you know? Nicky made his first team debut in November 1992, two months before he turned professional!

PAUL SCHOLES

2000/01 record:
40 (+ 4 sub) games, 12 goals

In the words of the song that can be heard at Old Trafford, he scores goals … and some great ones too! The pick of Paul's efforts in 2000/01 was actually a chip at the end of a terrific team move at Old Trafford, in which 32 passes were made to mesmerise Panathinaikos. He actually scored two goals in the last nine minutes that night, to turn a disappointing draw into a thrilling victory. And if that wasn't enough to make him unpopular with the Pana fans, he scored another last-minute goal against them in Athens, to save the Reds from an embarrassing defeat.

No wonder United fans love him, while opposition fans fear him. The other side can never feel comfortable when he's in or around their penalty area, because Paul can change the course of a game in an instant. He can also change people's opinions. Even former Liverpool players like Alan Hansen rate him, saying: 'Scholes is the only English player with world class technical ability. He is superb.'

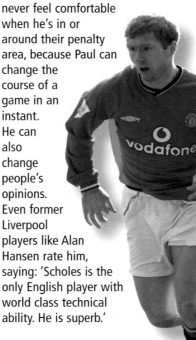

Did you know? Paul is the proud father of two children – son Arron and daughter Alicia.

ROY KEANE

2000/01 record:
43 games, 3 goals

Roy Keane's public rallying cries to the United crowd, and then to his team-mates, caused quite a stir during 2000/01. But really nobody should have been surprised, because the club captain has always worn his heart on his sleeve.

Of course, nobody is better qualified than Keano to talk about commitment and quality, because he simply oozes both whenever he pulls on his boots and leads the team onto the field. He was as inspirational as ever during 2000/01 whenever it came to digging in or driving the team forward, not only for his club but also for his country.

Roy's goals dried up slightly on the club scene, partly because he missed a few games after being sent off in the Charity Shield against Chelsea, and then the Manchester derby later in the season. But then if Keano doesn't score, he knows that others should. And if they don't deliver, well … they'll have the bellowing voice of their captain ringing in their ears!

Did you know? Roy Keane collected two Player of the Year awards before the first match of 2000/01. One was from the club's members, the other from the readers of Manchester United magazine.

EuroTrail

Sir Alex Ferguson's hunger for European glory didn't end with winning the UEFA Champions League Final in 1999. Ever since, Manchester United have been desperate to do it all again. Losing to Real Madrid in the year 2000 was a real blow, but it made the Reds all the more determined to succeed in 2001 …

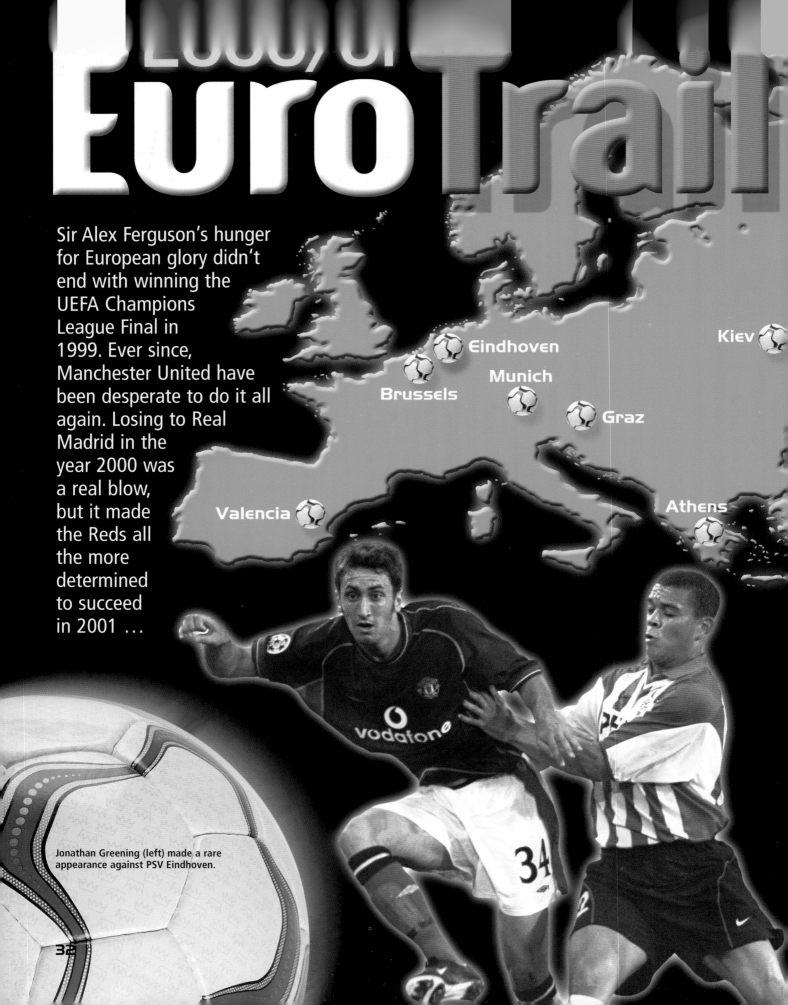

Brussels

Eindhoven

Munich

Graz

Kiev

Valencia

Athens

Jonathan Greening (left) made a rare appearance against PSV Eindhoven.

Yorke puts one in the back of the net against PSV Eindhoven.

United kicked off their UEFA Champions League campaign on home soil – and how! On a night when Denis Irwin's penalty gave the club their 200th goal in the competition, Andrew Cole's hat-trick made him Manchester United's record scorer in the European Cup. Teddy Sheringham also found the net in a fabulous 5–1 win over Anderlecht at Old Trafford.

United's defenders took their turn in the limelight in the next two games, in two very different ways! After keeping a clean sheet in Kiev against Dynamo (0–0), they caved in against PSV Eindhoven, losing the lead, after Paul Scholes had scored a second-minute penalty, and eventually losing the match 3–1.

Playing PSV in Manchester, Sheringham scored after eight minutes, but Van Bommel then equalised for Eindhoven. Luckily this time, Scholes and Yorke came to the rescue, but very late in the day – scoring in the 82nd and 87th minutes for the 3–1 win. Fergie's new quest for European glory was back on track, or was it?

Not quite. Losing 2–1 at Anderlecht on 24 October meant the Reds had to conquer Dynamo Kiev to reach the next round, and they just about managed it, 1–0, thanks to Sheringham scoring the all-important goal at Old Trafford.

In round two, the Reds stepped up a gear to beat Panathinaikos 3–1 at Old Trafford and then Sturm Graz 2–0 in Austria. There was a bit of a scare against the Greeks, who equalised, and Fabien had to work his mitts off to keep them out in the first half.

After a winter break in the Champions League, the Reds flew to sunny Spain to play Valencia. Well, it was sunny when they arrived; then the rain in Spain fell mainly on the Mestalla Stadium and made it a difficult game for both teams. 0–0 was a fair result, and a predictable one!

Not many people would have predicted Valencia's scorer when the sides met in Manchester six days later. Poor old Wesley Brown! He must have wished the ground would swallow him up, after his own-goal balanced out the early one in the right end by Andrew Cole. Whoops!

The 1–1 draw with Valencia kept United waiting for their place in the quarter-final, and so did the same result in the next match, away to Panathinaikos. Talk about doing things the hard way! Lucky for the Reds, the thirteenth of March offered them one last chance, and they took it by beating Sturm Graz 3–0 at home. The Austrians went out, and with them the Greeks. Now it was time to face the Germans again!

No one seemed surprised when Manchester United were drawn against Bayern Munich, but the Germans were delighted! It was the chance to take their revenge for losing the 1999 Final in the dying moments.

The first match, in Manchester, would be the high-pressure leg for United, who were expected to make a good start to the quarter-final tie on home soil. But things did not go according to plan. True, the Reds played well in the first forty-five minutes, but they couldn't find the cutting edge to beat Oliver Kahn, the Bayern goalkeeper.

In the second half, United's own number one, Fabien Barthez, made save after excellent save as the Germans started to take control. Eventually, they managed to break through when the Brazilian substitute, Paolo Sergio, scored the crucial away goal at Old Trafford. United 0, Bayern 1 – the Reds would have a mountain to climb in Munich.

What's more, they'd have to climb it without David Beckham, who was suspended for the second leg after picking up too many yellow cards. Their slack defending didn't help either. Another Brazilian, Giovane Elber, and the German international Mehmet Scholl made the score 2–0 in the first half to Bayern Munich, 3–0 on aggregate.

Although Ryan Giggs pulled one goal back, very soon after the break, it was still too little, too late. At the end of their 2–1 victory, the Bayern players celebrated their revenge as if they'd won the Cup itself.

The German club could look forward to the Champions League semi-finals, while United could only fly home to dream of a better run in the competition next time around, and who knows, maybe an appearance in the 2002 final in the home city of Sir Alex Ferguson. Glasgow, here we come … ?

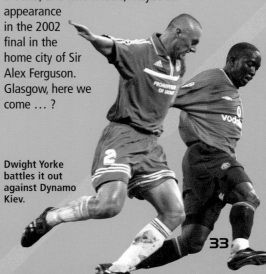

Dwight Yorke battles it out against Dynamo Kiev.

Group G Table	P	W	D	L	F	A	Pts
1 Anderlecht	6	4	0	2	11	14	12
2 Man United	6	3	1	2	11	7	10
3 PSV Eindhoven	6	3	0	3	9	9	9
4 Dynamo Kiev	6	1	1	4	7	8	4

Group A Table	P	W	D	L	F	A	Pts
1 Valencia CF	6	3	3	0	10	2	12
2 Man Utd	6	3	3	0	10	3	12
3 SK Sturm Graz	6	2	0	4	4	13	6
4 Panathinaikos	6	0	2	4	4	10	2

Super STRIKERS

Acrobatic goalkeepers, solid defences, battling midfielders and creative wingers are all well and good, but they'd be nowhere near the top of the league if they had no one to put the ball away! Strikers are still some of the most important and expensive players in the game.

DWIGHT YORKE

2000/01 record:
25 (+ 12 sub) games, 12 goals

If Dwight had a disappointing season, Arsenal would hate to see him on form! The Gunners would have been gob-smacked if they'd read some of the newspaper criticism of Yorkie, after his clinical performance against them at Old Trafford left them annihilated and embarrassed. All they saw of Dwight was a red blur, who whizzed past them three times in one half, one sunny February afternoon.

OK, so that was an extra-special day for Dwight – a one-off, some would say. But it proved that the talent which United had paid twelve million pounds for in 1998 had not mysteriously drained away from him. If anything had been drained, it was perhaps a little bit of energy during Dwight's flights to play for his country, Trinidad and Tobago. And maybe a touch of confidence, after the top scorer from 1999/2000 lost his regular place to Teddy Sheringham.

Whatever happened early on in the season, Dwight eventually came bouncing back and he scored two great goals against Coventry, on the day the Premiership title was actually won in 2000/01.

Did you know? Dwight's red card against Sunderland in the Worthington Cup was the first of his career. He's just not that kind of player!

TEDDY SHERINGHAM

2000/01 record:
32 (+ 10 sub) games, 21 goals

Like a classic car on the open road, Teddy purred through his final season with United, playing some of the best football of his life. He caught many people by surprise, especially those who thought he'd be sold before the original deal for Ruud van Nistelrooy fell through. When the young Dutchman went back to Holland to recover from his injury, the Englishman just pounced on the opportunity and was voted Player of the Year by the PFA and the Football Writers Association.

Fifteen goals in the Premiership, including a hat-trick against Southampton, five goals in the Champions League and one in the FA Cup at Fulham added up to a tremendous season for Ted, who also forced his way back into the England squad. It was a case of if you're good enough, you're still young enough: not long after turning 35 in April 2001, Sheri scored his 21st goal of the season, a cool penalty in the heat of the derby match against Manchester City.

Did you know? Teddy played his first and last league games for United against Tottenham Hotspur, who re-signed him in May 2001.

OLE GUNNAR SOLSKJAER

2000/01 record:
25 (+ 21 sub) games, 13 goals

Ole was unlucky enough to play the super-sub role again in 2000/01, while his 13 goals were just unlucky for other teams! The 13th one, which he scored as a sub against Charlton, was a vital one, because it revitalised United after they lost to Liverpool and then Bayern Munich.

Not even Ole Gunnar could grab a goal against the Germans this time, two years after he'd torn apart their European Cup dreams in the Nou Camp. Instead he had to settle for helping the Reds to win another title, and finishing joint second in the scoring charts behind Sheringham.

He scored in all three English competitions, including two goals in the Worthington Cup at Watford, when he was one of the oldest players on display. Nobody could call him Baby Face any more, but he was still an assassin, especially in December and January.

In those cold winter months, he drilled home six goals in seven games, including decisive ones against Ipswich and Aston Villa.

The Norwegian obviously has a nose for goal and a sharp brain which impresses even United's all-time record goal scorer, Sir Bobby Charlton, who says: 'I don't know anybody who makes up his mind quicker than him.'

Did you know? Sir Alex Ferguson has described Ole Gunnar as 'the best substitute ever'.

seven deadly wins

Just one word could be used to describe the way Manchester United won their seventh Premiership title –

AWESOME!

Over the course of 38 matches, the rampant Reds were far too consistent for their nearest rivals from Arsenal, Leeds and Liverpool. But which were the key games in which the Champions really turned on the style? We've selected the best seven samples of United's Premiership power. We hope you agree.

Bradford City, 6–0

Cole (11)
Fortune (23, 60)
Sheringham (71, 81)
Beckham (85)
**Tuesday, 5 September 2000,
8 pm, Old Trafford**

This was Quinton Fortune's lucky night, and his name would have been all over the newspapers if Teddy Sheringham hadn't scored two as well! Skipper for the night, Sheri scored in the 71st and 81st minutes, after Andrew Cole's opener and Fortune's double had put the Reds 3–0 up inside the first hour. David Beckham played in his favourite position, centre midfield, and celebrated this with a super solo goal to make it 6–0!

Leeds United, 3–0

Yorke (41)
Beckham (50)
Jones own-goal (83)
**Saturday, 21 October 2000
11.30 am, Old Trafford**

Both teams were missing star players, but only one team was ever going to win. Dwight Yorke scored first for the Reds, not long after David Beckham replaced the injured captain Roy Keane. Perhaps Becks fancied his chances as United's new super-sub because he bagged one himself in the second half. Goal number three was a gift from Leeds man Matthew Jones, who cracked under pressure to put the ball in his own net.

Southampton, 5–0

Cole (9, 73)
Sheringham (45, 51, 55)
**Saturday, 28 October 2000
3 pm, Old Trafford**

If the Saints marched in dreaming of another 3-3 draw like the year before, Teddy Sheringham soon woke them up. On this fantastic form, the super-striker could score in his sleep! Not counting half-time, he actually netted three goals in ten minutes. The first was a superb chip over the head of Paul Jones, who'd earlier let Andrew Cole's shot slip through his body. Andrew finished 'em off when he nodded in the fifth.

West Ham United, 3–1

Solskjaer (3)
Pearce own-goal (33)
Yorke (57)
**Monday, 1 January 2001
8 pm, Old Trafford**

United welcomed in the New Year with a happy hour of football against the unhappy Hammers. Ole Gunnar Solskjaer drilled in the first goal after just three minutes when he stopped Rigobert Song from dribbling out of trouble. Pressing ever forward, the Reds made their own luck when Stuart Pearce's boot deflected Phil Neville's shot into the net. Dwight Yorke's diving header killed the game off, long before Kanoute's consolation in the 72nd minute.

Sunderland, 1–0

Cole (46)
**Wednesday, 31 January 2001
7.45 pm, Stadium of Light**

Not all the big wins are high-scoring! This was an important result for United, coming just three days after West Ham knocked them out of the FA Cup at Old Trafford. The Champions passed a tough character test to become the first away team to win at Sunderland's ground all season. Not even three players being sent off (United's scorer Cole, plus Gray and Rae from the home side) could divert them from their business.

Arsenal, 6–1

Yorke (3,18,21)
Keane (26)
Solskjaer (35)
Sheringham (90)
**Sunday, 25 February 2001
1 pm, Old Trafford**

What an amazing game! This classic win for United has been captured on a video that Reds fans are sure to watch again and again, especially for the first forty-five minutes when the Champions went 5–1 up. This was a dream match for Dwight Yorke, who scored a hat-trick in eighteen minutes to make his critics eat their words. Roy, Ole and Teddy also scored on an embarrassing afternoon for Arsenal, United's nearest rivals.

Coventry City, 4–2

Yorke (13, 27)
Giggs (82)
Scholes (87)
**Saturday, 14 April 2001
12 pm, Old Trafford**

Whatever the kick-off time, and whatever the weather, United are natural winners. Three hours after this match ended, they were Champions. By then, it was pouring down in Manchester, and the fans had already gone home, buzzing after a brilliant game. Hartson (11,33) and Yorke both scored twice in the first half, before the match was settled by a pinpoint strike from Scholes and by Ryan's looping header, United's 100th goal of the successful season.

**Dwight gets it right!
Yorke celebrates his hat trick against Arsenal.**

Red Letters Quiz

Welcome to the easiest quiz in the Manchester United annual! In fact, it's as easy as A-B-C ... or at least it should be, because we've supplied you with all the answers! Here they are:

Fabien Barthez; Gary Neville; Denis Irwin; Ronny Johnsen; Jaap Stam; David Beckham; Nicky Butt; Andrew Cole; Ryan Giggs; Phil Neville; Roy Keane; Raimond van der Gouw; Paul Scholes; Dwight Yorke; Ole Gunnar Solskjaer; Ronnie Wallwork; Wes Brown; Quinton Fortune; Bojan Djordjic; Mikael Silvestre; Michael Stewart; John O'Shea; Luke Chadwick; Ruud van Nistelrooy; Steve McClaren; Sir Alex Ferguson.

All you have to do is match the answers to the right questions, so that every one of the 26 Manchester United players and coaches in our list is attached to a letter of the alphabet. There's no sharing, it's one letter per person, please!

As for the order in which you answer the questions, that's up to you. It might be a good idea to start with the ones you know straight away, remembering to cross out the names to narrow down your options for the more difficult questions. Have fun, and when you're done, the answers are on page 60.

A is for ... Anderlecht.
Who scored a hat-trick against them at Old Trafford?

B is for ... Besiktas (FC).
Who left them to join United?

C is for ... Coventry City.
Who scored two goals against them in April 2000?

D is for ... derby match.
Who scored in the Manchester derby at Maine Road in November 2000?

E is for ... Edgeley Park, Stockport.
Who played for Stockport on loan?

F is for ... FA Cup Final.
Who missed it through suspension in 1999?

G is for ... Goodison Park.
Who scored United's first goal there in 2000/01?

H is for ... Hull City.
Who used to play for them?

I is for ... Inter Milan.
Who left them to join United?

J is for ... Juventus.
Who scored against them in 1997 and 1999?

K is for ... Kristiansund.
Who was born there in 1973?

L is for ... Leeds United.
Who scored at their ground in March 2001?

M is for ... Manchester City.
Who was sent off against them in 2001?

N is for ... Newcastle.
Who made his debut against them in 1999?

O is for ... Oss.
Who was born there?

P is for ... penalty.
Who scored one against PSV Eindhoven?

Q is for ... Queen's Park.
Who used to play for them?

R is for ... Royal Antwerp.
Who played on loan for them in 2001?

S is for ... Sweden.
Who plays international football for them?

T is for ... Toulouse (FC).
Who started his career with them?

U is for ... UEFA Cup.
Who made his debut in that competition?

V is for ... Valencia.
Who scored an own-goal for them in 2001?

W is for ... Watford.
Who made his debut there in 2000?

X is for ... XVII.
Who wore that squad number in 2000/01?

Y is for ... Youth Cup.
Who lifted the trophy as captain in 1995?

Z is for ... Zwolle (FC).
Who used to play for them?

It's a DATE!

JANUARY	FEBRUARY	MARCH	APRIL	MAY	JUNE
1 Tuesday	**1** Friday		**1** Monday	**1** Wednesday	**1** Saturday
2 Wednesday	**2** Saturday		**2** Tuesday	**2** Thursday	**2** Sunday
3 Thursday	**3** Sunday		**3** Wednesday	**3** Friday	**3** Monday
	4 Monday		**4** Thursday		
	5 Tuesday				
	6 Wednesday				
	7 Thursday		**8**		
	8 Friday		**9**		**9** Sunday
	9 Saturday		**10**		**10** Monday
	10 Sunday		**11** Th		**11** Tuesday
	Monday		**12** Fri		**12** Wednesday
	Tuesday		**13** Sat		**13** Thursday
	Wednesday		**14** Su		**14** Friday
	Thursday		**15** Mond		**15** Saturday
	ay		**16** Tuesday		**16** Sunday
	rday	**17** Sunda			**17** Monday
	18 Monday	**18** Monday			**18** Tuesday
19 Saturday	**19** Tuesday	**19** Tuesda			
20 Sunday	**20** Wednesday	**20** Wedn		**20** Monday	
21 Monday	**21** Thursday	**21** Thurs		**21** Tuesday	
	22 Friday	**22** Frida		**22** Wednesday	
	23 Saturday	**23** Sat			
	24 Sunday	**24 Su**			June
	25 Monday	**25** M			
	26 Tuesday	**26** Tuesday			**25**
	27 Wednesday	**27** Wednesd			**26**
	28 Thursday	**28** Thursday			**27**
		29 Friday			**28** Friday
		30 Saturday			**29** Saturday
		31 Sunday			**30 Sunday**

January

Happy birthday to — **Nicky Butt** and **Phil Neville**, on the same day, the 21st! Nicholas, aged 27, will have two more candles to snuff out than Philip.

Two years ago, United played in the very first FIFA Club World Championships, over in red-hot Rio de Janeiro. It wasn't a great tournament for the lads (Corinthians won it) but at least they were able to play in Brazil's legendary **Maracana Stadium**. Top place!

February

Many happy returns to — **Gary Neville** and **Ole Gunnar Solskjaer**. Gaz celebrates first, he was born in Bury on 18th February 1975. Ole was born in 1973, on 26th February.

Three years ago, **Ole Gunnar** blasted four goals past big Dave Beasant, as the rampant Reds set a new record away win for the Premiership. Nottingham Forest 1, Manchester United 8 was the first game watched by Fergie's new assistant, **Steve McClaren**.

April

Happy birthday to — **Teddy Sheringham**. 1966 was a great year for English football, because SuperTed was born in Highams Park, London. Raise a glass to Sheri on the 2nd, even if he is a Spurs player!

Ten years ago, **Fergie** won only his second trophy as United boss. The Reds, dressed in a strange blue and white strip, beat Nottingham Forest (them again!) 1-0 in the Rumbelows Cup Final. It's better known as the League Cup to **Giggsy** and **Denis**, who both played that day at Wembley Stadium.

March

Hartelijk gefeliciteerd to — **Raimond van der Gouw**. The ace Dutch goalkeeper will be... ssssh, best whisper it, 39 on the 24th. Don't worry, Rai, my dad reckons life starts at 40!

Five years ago, **Ryan Giggs** produced one of the best performances of his career, to help United destroy Porto 4-0 at Old Trafford in the Champions League quarter-final. The Welsh wizard scored one of the goals and caused all sorts of problems for the poor old Portuguese defenders.

May

Happy birthday to — **David Beckham** and **Quinton Fortune**. Becks was born to proud parents Ted and Sandra on 2nd May in 1975. Mr Fortune's first day, 21st May 1977, was also a lucky one for United — they carried home the FA Cup after beating Liverpool!

Nine years ago, United won their first League title under **Sir Alex**. The club had waited since 1967 to be called Champions again, so they were in no hurry to give it up... they won it again the following May. And in 1996, and in 1997, 1999, 2000, 2001... keep it up, lads!

June

Joyeux anniversaire to — **Fabien Barthez**. The French goalkeeper first dribbled out of his area on 28th June 1971. **Ronny Johnsen** is another June baby, so let's wish him a happy 33rd birthday on the 10th.

Five years ago, United signed **Teddy Sheringham** from Spurs. The England striker was under pressure to replace **Eric Cantona**, but clever as ever, Ted asked Fergie if he could wear the number ten shirt instead of the King's number seven. Smart move!

2002

is set to be another important year for Manchester United. The Reds will have to find a new manager when Sir Alex Ferguson retires in May; in the summer, the team's international players will hope to be playing in the World Cup Finals in Japan and Korea. Then, in September, the club will celebrate a very special birthday – the 100th birthday of Manchester United! Wonder if the Queen will send them a telegram? Who knows, but maybe you could send a card or two to your favourite players at Old Trafford, using this extra special calendar.

JULY	AUGUST	SEPTEMBER	OCTOBER	NOVEMBER	DECEMBER

July

...gefeliciteerd to – **Jaap Stam**. ...p sat on his mother's lap for the very ...time on 17th July 1972.

...years ago, United splashed out £3.75 ...on to sign **Roy Keane** from ...ingham Forest. The transfer fee was then ...record for the club, but the Irishman was ...orth every penny!

August

Happy birthday to – **Roy Keane**. The captain's first kick in the open air took place in Cork, on 10th August 1971. Six years later, **Mikael Silvestre** followed suit. Joyeux anniversaire to Mik for the 9th.

Ten years ago, United played their first-ever fixture in the brand new Premier League, and lost 2-1 to Sheffield United. Not a great start but the Reds soon adjusted to the new competition. See May!

September

Happy birthday – to **Manchester United, 100 years old on Friday 6th September!** That's the anniversary of the club's first match, after changing its name from Newton Heath in 1902.

Ten years ago, **Gary Neville** and **David Beckham** made their first team debuts for United. Nev beat Becks to it by seven days, playing in the UEFA Cup against Torpedo Moscow on 16th September. Like a lot of young Reds, David made his debut in the League Cup, this time at Brighton on 23rd September 1992.

October

Happy birthday – to **Wes Brown, Andrew Cole and Denis Irwin**. The 13th was lucky for Wesley, born in 1979, while Andrew arrived in Nottingham on the 15th in 1971. Den has had a few fancy dress birthdays over the years, he celebrates his 37th birthday on Hallowe'en.

Five years ago, one of the best-ever European matches at **Old Trafford** took place on 1st October 1997. Juventus scored in the first and last minutes, but in between United netted with Teddy's towering header, a super strike by Scholes and a great goal by Giggs. Final score: United 3 Juventus 2. Top drawer!

November

Penblwydd hapus – to **Ryan Giggs**, who came into this world in Cardiff on 29th November 1973. It's a good month for attacking talent at Old Trafford – **Dwight Yorke** parties on the 3rd and **Luke Chadwick** follows him on the 18th. In the middle, **Paul Scholes** will hope to celebrate his birthday with a goal on Saturday 16th. Many happy returns to them all.

Three years ago, on 30 November 1999, United won the Inter-Continental Cup for the very first time, when they beat Palmeiras, the champions of South America, in Tokyo, Japan. **Roy Keane** scored the only goal, but **Ryan Giggs** was the man-of-the-match. His reward? A brand new car!

December

Many happy returns – to **Sir Alex Ferguson**, who has two reasons to celebrate on New Year's Eve. Here's to a relaxing 61st birthday, Boss, and all the best for your retirement.

Eight years ago – **David Beckham** made his Champions League debut and scored his first goal for the Reds at Old Trafford on 7th December 1994. Galatasaray were the opponents, but the Turkish delight was all United's in a superb 4-0 win.

WE'RE RED

Tracking the 2001/02 campaign

The 2001/02 season will be another manic one for Manchester United, with the team chasing honours on four fronts in the hope of giving **Sir Alex Ferguson** a fantastic farewell party. With the special charts on these three pages, you can keep your own record of this important campaign in the FA Barclaycard Premiership, the UEFA Champions League, the FA Cup sponsored by AXA and the Worthington (League) Cup.

FA Premiership Fixtures

MATCH DATE	SCORE REDS THEM	OPPOSITION AND VENUE	SCORERS	POINTS THIS MATCH	TOTAL	LEAGUE POSITION

02 2001 2 AND READY!
2001 2
Premiership • FA • Europe • League Cup

MATCH DATE	SCORE REDS	THEM	OPPOSITION AND VENUE	SCORERS	POINTS THIS MATCH	TOTAL	LEAGUE POSITION

FA Cup Matches

MATCH DATE	SCORE REDS	THEM	OPPOSITION AND VENUE	SCORERS	ROUND

League Cup Matches

MATCH DATE	SCORE REDS	THEM	OPPOSITION AND VENUE	SCORERS	ROUND

UEFA Champions League Matches

MATCH DATE	SCORE REDS	THEM	OPPOSITION AND VENUE	SCORERS	POINTS THIS MATCH	TOTAL	GROUP POSITION
							Q-F
							Q-F
							S-F
							S-F
							Final

First Phase / *Second Phase*

Squad Changes

PLAYER'S NAME	POSITION	MOVING TO/FROM	NUMBER	IN	OUT	FEE OR FREE	GOOD OR BAD MOVE
Teddy Sheringham	Forward	Tottenham	10	x	✓	Free	OK

How it all started

1889

1904-5

2002 will be a very
special year for the
Reds, because it will be the 100th
year of Manchester United. The club
first played under that name on 6
September 1902, but what were
they called before then? And how
did the first team get together? For
answers to these questions, and a
few others, read on …

On the right track
The first 'United' players were actually
workers in the Carriage and Wagon
department of the Lancashire and Yorkshire
Railway. They formed a football team in
1878, calling themselves Newton Heath LYR
and playing on a pitch in North Road, near
to their railway yard.

Local heroes
Newton Heath proved they were a good
team when they entered the Manchester
Cup, a competition for all football clubs in
the city and the surrounding area. They won
the Cup in 1886, and finished as runners-up
in 1885 and 1887. The railway bosses were
so impressed, they gave the players time
off to train!

Time for a new challenge
Bored with local football and friendlies, the
Heathens entered the national Football
League in 1892. Robert Donaldson scored
their first league goal but they still lost
their first game, 4–3 at Blackburn. The club
didn't win until their seventh match, when
Donaldson scored a hat-trick in the 10–1
thrashing of Wolves!

Moving home
The Heathens hoped that moving to a new
ground at Bank Street, Clayton, would bring
them better luck. Sadly the air was polluted
by factory fumes, and the pitch had more
sand on it than grass. When Walsall played
there, they complained so much that their
14–1 defeat was later wiped from the
records!

Dog to the rescue
Struggling for money in the Second
Division, Newton Heath decided to hold a
fund-raising fair that opened on 27
February 1901. The club struck lucky when
the St Bernard dog belonging to captain
Harry Stafford escaped from the show and
was found by the wealthy owner of a local
brewery, John Henry Davies …

New money, new name
Mr Davies and Mr Stafford saved the club
in 1902 when Newton Heath went
bankrupt. Davies became club president,
while a man called Louis Rocca suggested a
new name – Manchester United. The new
team won their first match, against
Gainsborough Trinity, won the League in
1908, the FA Cup in 1909 and moved to
Old Trafford in 1910. **So now you know!**

A long, long time ago … this is how
the United teams and Old Trafford itself
used to look.

1892-3

FUTURE FACES

Many years after Beckham, Butt, Giggs and Co. came bursting through into the first team, the club is still producing its own players. Here are just four of the young faces who could soon be wearing the famous red shirt week in, week out …

RONNIE WALLWORK

2000/01 record:
6 (+ 10 sub) games, 0 goals

Ronnie seems to have been around for ages, but really he's still a young player patiently waiting for a regular place in the United first team. He came close to his goal, early on in 2000/01, when he started two of the first four games and played very well in central defence alongside Stam and Johnsen. Ronnie returned to his seat on the bench when the injured senior players returned, but he came on often enough to add to the experience that he had picked up on loan with clubs like Carlisle United, Stockport County and Royal Antwerp. He also started some senior matches in midfield towards the end of the season, as Sir Alex Ferguson offered the fans a sneak preview of how the Reds might line up in the future. If the next manager of Manchester United was taking notes, he'll know already that he can rely on Ronnie.

Did you know? United beat Barnsley 7–0 in Ronnie's debut match, in October 1997. Not a bad start!

MICHAEL STEWART

2000/01 record:
3 (+ 2 sub) games, 0 goals

Sir Alex Ferguson might have a felt a twinge of national pride when Michael Stewart, his fellow Scot, made his breakthrough into the first team during 2000/01. The flame-haired midfielder made his debut in the Worthington (League) Cup, Fergie's favourite competition for giving young players their first taste of senior football. The boy from Edinburgh did well, as substitute at both Watford and Sunderland, and later in the season he did even better. He started the Premiership match at Middlesbrough, in the place of his injured role model Roy Keane, and demonstrated some similarities to the great captain in the powerful way he played the game. Michael also started the next League game against Derby County at Old Trafford, where he collected the award as Reserve Team Player of the Year 2001. It was richly deserved and a sign of more to come.

Did you know? Michael is an Under-21 international and has also trained with the senior Scotland squad.

BOJAN DJORDJIC

2000/01 record:
0 (+ 1 sub) games, 0 goals

People used to say Ryan Giggs was like the new George Best. But could Bojan, in turn, be the new Ryan? United fans were probably wondering that when the boy born in Belgrade scored a great Giggs-like goal on live television in May 2001. Receiving a pass to feet inside the Celtic half, he moved forward to float the ball over the goalkeeper's head and wrap up a win for United in Tommy Boyd's testimonial match. It was Boyd's big night, but Bojan's too by the final whistle. It came just twelve months after the winger picked up an award from the club's coaching staff, as United's Young Player of the Year 2000. Not a bad start for the lad who left his family home in Sweden to try his luck overseas!

Did you know? Bojan's father, Branko Djordjic, used to play for Red Star Belgrade and Yugoslavia.

JOHN O'SHEA

2000/01 record:
2 games, 0 goals

The gentle giant is in one of United's longest queues for a first team place. But after playing on loan for Bournemouth in 2000, and Royal Antwerp in 2001, Big John could soon jump over a few of his rivals and take up one of the two centre-half positions. His appearances in England's Nationwide League and Belgium's First Division will have toughened him up and added the competitive edge to his game, and he's also gaining experience by playing for the Republic of Ireland Under-21s. After struggling to score against Johnsen, Brown and Stam, opposing strikers could be in for some more misery if John O'Shea has his way!

Did you know? John is 190 centimetres tall, the same height as Jaap Stam and Rai van der Gouw.

Record-breaking REDS

To sign the best forwards, you have to spend big money, and sometimes that means breaking transfer records as well as the bank! Sir Alex Ferguson has twice broken the British transfer record by signing a striker – here we profile the two men in question, who arrived at Old Trafford six years apart …

ANDREW COLE

2000/01 record:
26 (+ 4 sub) games, 13 goals

Andrew was the subject of one of the most sensational transfers ever, when the best team in the country bought the best forward for £6.25 million in January 1995.

The fee was then a record for the British transfer market, but it seemed money well spent when the former Newcastle United hotshot scored five goals in Manchester United's 9–0 thrashing of Ipswich Town! The end of the season raised a few questions, though, when the Reds ran out of luck and Blackburn won the title instead. The top scorer for Blackburn, Alan Shearer, later replaced Andrew as England's most expensive striker when he joined Newcastle for £15 million!

Of course, in the years since then, Andrew has won many more honours than Shearer, including the Double and the Treble! And in all cases, Cole's goals have proved vital to the United cause. In 1998/99, for example, he scored the goal against Tottenham that clinched the Premiership title, and the winner in Turin when United beat Juventus in the Champions League semi-final.

While helping United to complete a hat-trick of League titles in 1999, 2000 and 2001, Cole has also claimed some personal milestones. During the 1999/2000 season, he scored the 100th goal of his United career in the 2–2 draw at Wimbledon. In the following campaign, Andrew overtook Denis Law as the club's all-time top scorer in the European Cup when he bagged a hat-trick at home to Anderlecht. That took his tally for the competition up to 17 – and he later made it 18 with a goal against Valencia.

The only disappointment about Cole's career is the low number of caps he's earned for his country. But after basically being ignored by several different England managers, the United striker has started well under Sven Goran Eriksson. Andrew will always remember Albania with affection, because that's where he scored his first international goal in March 2001, in the last few seconds of his 13th appearance.

Did you know? Andrew's son and daughter celebrate their birthdays in the same month. Devante was born on 10 May 1995, the same day that dad scored against Southampton, and Faith was born on 9 May 2001.

RUUD VAN NISTELROOY

2000/01 record:
8 (+ 2 sub) games, 4 goals (for PSV Eindhoven)

When Ruud goes head-to-head against Leeds defender Rio Ferdinand in 2001/02, it will be the most expensive duel ever seen in English football, with the two players together worth £37 million!

The record amount of cash United spent on Ruud, £19 million, sounds even more amazing in Dutch currency – 67 million guilders! But the goal-scoring wizard from Oss insists he's not worried about the fee. In fact, he feels it will boost

his confidence, knowing that United were prepared to spend so much money on him.

Ruud also knows the Reds had been raving about him for some time! Sir Alex Ferguson first heard of his talents in 1998, just before he left Heerenveen to join PSV Eindhoven. And van Nistelrooy would have joined United in time for 2000/01 if he hadn't suffered a serious knee injury.

That cruel stroke of misfortune forced the Reds to call off the transfer in April 2000, but they kept in touch with Ruud as he recovered back home in Holland. It was a long road of rehab for the striker but he showed patience and courage along the way, and by March 2001 he was banging in the goals again for PSV. After seeing him in action several times, United moved in for their man once again, with chief executive Peter Kenyon striking a new deal for Ruud with PSV president Harry Van Raaj.

This time van Nistelrooy's dream transfer came true, and two days after flying to England to meet the fans and the press, he celebrated by scoring a header for Holland in their 4–0 win over Cyprus. Ruud then finished the 2000/01 season by helping PSV to win the Dutch league, the perfect ending to his days in Eindhoven. Let's hope his days in England are every bit as successful. Welcome, Ruud!

Did you know? Ruud officially became a Manchester United player on his 25th birthday, 1 July 2001.

Here's a fun thing to do, using a pen, some sellotape or glue and your favourite picture of yourself playing football. The aim of the activity is to make your own player profile, and to give you some idea of how it should look, here's one we made earlier for Manchester United's young wing wizard Luke Chadwick.

Make your own

Full name: Luke Harry Chadwick

Birth date: 18 November 1980

Birth place: Cambridge

Height: 180 cm

Weight: 67 kg

Current team: Manchester United

Former teams: Melbourn Village College; Cambridge & District Schoolboys; Cambridgeshire County; Melbourn Tigers; Eternit Colts; Arsenal Schoolboys; Royal Antwerp (on loan)

Position: Right or left wing

Favourite other position: Centre forward (my old position)

Who's your best friend in the squad? I get on really well with the young players like Wes Brown, Michael Stewart and Ronnie Wallwork. We all sit together on the bus.

Who's the best player you've ever played with? People like Beckham, Giggs and Keane, to name a few. Then there's Cole, Yorke … there are so many great players in our squad, I couldn't pick out just one.

What job would you have done if you hadn't made the grade as a footballer? I've never really thought about it! Anything outdoors to do with sport would have been nice, like PE teacher or groundsman.

What's the worst bit about training? I enjoy training all the time, it's great fun. Except maybe the running at the end of a session, the stamina work!

What is your favourite away ground? The Charleroi ground in Belgium. That's a great stadium, I really enjoyed playing there when I was with Royal Antwerp. The Stadium of Light (Sunderland) is probably the best one in England I've played at.

Describe the best goal of your career. I remember scoring a good goal for Melbourn Village College when we won the schools cup final. I went around a couple of players, hit the ball with my left foot and it went right in the top corner. It pulled us back to 2-2 in the match and we went on to win 3-2.

What has been the best performance of your career so far? It was against Watford in the Worthington Cup! That was a big performance for me because it helped to keep me in the first team squad for the rest of the season.

What are your ambitions and dreams? To play as many times as I can for Manchester United because I love the team, and to play for England. That's what I dream of and hopefully one day that will happen!

PLAYER PROFILE

Full name:

Birth date:

Birth place:

Height:

Weight:

Current team:

Former teams:

Position:

Favourite other position:

Who's your best friend in the squad?

Who's the best player you've played against?

Who's the best player you've ever played with?

What job would you like to do if you don't make the grade as a footballer?

What's the worst bit about training?

What is your favourite away ground?

Describe the best goal of your career.

What has been the best performance of your career so far?

What are your ambitions and dreams?

Stick down your own photograph here.

This player looks Red Hot to me!

JEEPERS KEEPERS!
JEEPERS KEEPERS!
JEEPERS KEEPERS!
JEEPERS KEEPERS!
JEEPERS
JEEPERS KEEPERS!
JEEPERS KEEPERS!
JEEPERS KEEPERS!

Many hands make light work, but when Peter Schmeichel retired, many men made hard work of replacing him! In the two seasons after the Great Dane departed, Manchester United used seven different goalkeepers in the first team. Everyone knows Fabien Barthez is now the number one, but what about the other six?

MARK BOSNICH

Born: Sydney, Australia, 13 January 1972

The first brave man to step into Schmeichel's shoes (and gloves) was Mark Bosnich. Perhaps it was a case of better the (red) devil you know, because the Australian had already played three games for United, during his student days in Manchester. He rejoined the Treble-winning Reds in the summer of '99, but if he

thought it'd be plain sailing to silverware, he was soon given a kick up the shorts. August was a nightmare, with United losing the Charity Shield to Arsenal, and then Bosnich losing his place through injury. Although he returned to help the Reds win the Toyota Cup in Tokyo and the Premiership title, it was goodbye Bosnich from the moment they signed Barthez. He later joined Chelsea on a free transfer.

Best game? Bosnich played a blinder in Tokyo, and against Real in Madrid (1999/2000 season).
Nightmare? Losing his place in the team.

RAIMOND van der GOUW

Born: Oldenzaal, Holland, 24 March 1963

The misfortunes of Mark Bosnich opened the door once more for Rai van der Gouw, the original man behind Schmeichel. Rai didn't expect to play very much when he first joined United in 1996. After all, he was only there to cover for the world's greatest goalkeeper. But as the seasons wore on, Rai found himself involved more and more until finally, in the 1999/2000 season, he went head-to-head with Bosnich for the job of first-choice keeper. Schmeichel had gone by then, so really it was up to Rai to stake his claim. He was doing just that when the outstretched leg of Martin Keown took Rai and the ball over the line in injury time at Arsenal. No equalising goal was given but ouch, that hurt! Luckily Rai soon recovered, and in the season 2000/01 he was back doing what he does best, filling in for Fabien Barthez.

Best game? Made some great saves against Sturm Graz in 1999/2000.
Nightmare? Pushing the ball into his own net in Bordeaux (1999/2000).

Two more keepers who played in 1999/2000 were **Nick Culkin** (below left), who made a brief debut at Arsenal, and **Massimo Taibi** (right), who failed to live up to his dazzling debut match.

JEEPERS KEEPERS!

PAUL RACHUBKA

Born: San Luis Obispo, USA, 21 May 1981

With Taibi's career in tatters and Culkin out on loan, Sir Alex asked Rachubka to be his third-choice goalkeeper at the FIFA Club World Championship. Consequently, the California-born keeper who was raised in Stockport made his senior debut in Brazil, in the very famous Maracana Stadium. OK, so he was playing against South Melbourne, not Socrates, Romario or Pele, but even so, it was a fantastic moment for the boy who once cleaned Peter Schmeichel's boots, when he came on in the 83rd minute for Rai van der Gouw. Rachubka's next game in the first team was in the lower profile setting of a Worthington Cup tie at Watford, where he came on as sub for Rai again. He made his first-ever start later against Leicester in 2000/01 after Barthez pulled a muscle in the warm-up.

Best game? Kept a clean sheet in his first full appearance, United 2, Leicester City 0 (2000/01).

Nightmare? Too young for any sleepless nights at the moment.

ANDY GORAM

Born: Bury, England, 13 April 1964

In March 2001, Sir Alex Ferguson found himself facing some important fixtures without his two senior goalkeepers. This time he solved the problem by going back to his roots to sign Andy Goram, whom he'd first picked for Scotland sixteen years earlier! The former Oldham, Rangers, Hibs and Motherwell goalkeeper made his debut in the title-winning match against Coventry, and stayed in the squad until the end of the season to provide experienced cover, advice ... even a few laughs. You can always expect those from a goalkeeper, especially one who's seen as much action.

Goodbye GAFFER

Sir Alex Ferguson's glorious reign as Manchester United manager will come to an end in May 2002, hopefully in the UEFA Champions League final at Hampden Park – the ground where he started his football career as a Queen's Park player. That would certainly be a fitting finale for the man who has brought so much success to Old Trafford during his sixteen seasons in charge. Here we remember the first fifteen …

1986/87
11th place in League

1987/88
League runners-up

1988/89
11th place in League

1989/90
FA Cup winners

The season when Alex was almost sacked! That was what the newspapers thought, anyway, as poor league form saw the Reds finish thirteenth. They even lost 5–1 to Manchester City! Luckily, they played much better in the FA Cup, and won Fergie's first honour as United boss when they beat Crystal Palace in the final.

1990/91
European Cup Winners' Cup winners, League Cup runners-up

The Reds reached two finals in 1991. They lost the League Cup to Sheffield Wednesday 1–0 at Wembley, but beat Barcelona in Rotterdam 2–1 to win the Cup Winners' Cup. The European success completed a double for Fergie, as he had lifted the same trophy with Aberdeen in 1983.

1991/92
League Cup winners, European Super Cup winners, League runners-up

The season in which Ryan Giggs became a first team regular saw United lose the title by only four points to Leeds. Fergie won the second trophy of his reign when the Reds returned to the League Cup final, this time beating Nottingham Forest 1–0.

1992/93
League Champions

Bravo! United finally won the League Championship, for the first time since 1967. Fergie's masterstroke was the signing of Eric Cantona from Leeds United, midway through the season. The Frenchman scored and created some wonderful goals for the Reds.

1993/94
League Champions, FA Cup winners, League Cup runners-up

Fergie made history when he became the first United manager to win the Double. His team beat Blackburn Rovers in the title race and thrashed Chelsea 4–0 in the FA Cup final at Wembley. The Reds almost won England's first-ever treble, but they failed when they lost the League Cup final 3–1 to Aston Villa.

1994/95
League runners-up, FA Cup runners-up

1995/96
League Champions, FA Cup winners

The historic 'Double Double' was achieved with the help of some promising young players. Fergie brought David Beckham, Nicky Butt, Gary and Phil Neville, and Paul Scholes into his first team, as United saw off the title challenge of Newcastle and beat Liverpool 1–0 in the FA Cup final with a great, late goal by captain Cantona.

1996/97
League Champions

New signings Ole Gunnar Solskjaer, Rai van der Gouw and Ronny Johnsen all played their part as United again won the Premiership race ahead of Newcastle. But there was disappointment for Fergie when Borussia Dortmund defeated his team in the European Cup semi-finals, and Eric Cantona announced he was retiring.

1997/98
League runners-up

1998/99
League Champions, FA Cup winners, European Cup winners

Wow! Fergie spent lots of money on Blomqvist, Stam and Yorke, and was richly rewarded with a remarkable Treble. The Reds came from behind to sink Spurs 2–1 and win the League, and defeated Newcastle 2–0 to lift the FA Cup. Then, in the dying seconds of the season, Sheringham and Solskjaer scored to win the European Cup final 2–1, at the expense of heartbroken Bayern Munich. Amazing!

1999/2000
League Champions, Inter-Continental Cup winners

Fergie's men entered FIFA's first Club World Championship, instead of the FA Cup, but came home empty-handed from boiling hot Brazil. The break from the English winter helped them to recharge their batteries though, as they won the title by a mile. Winning the Inter-Continental Cup in Tokyo was a special bonus.

2000/01
League Champions

After signing Fabien Barthez, United won the title again with ease, this time wrapping it up on Easter Saturday when they beat Coventry, and Arsenal lost to Middlesbrough. It meant that Sir Alexander Chapman Ferguson was the first manager ever to win three titles in a row in England.

But can Fergie make it four in a row? We'll find out in May 2002 ...

Meet the Backroom BOYS

If the **Manchester United** movie, 'Beyond The Promised Land', had been nominated for the Oscars, these guys would have been big contenders for the award of Best Supporting Actor!

From dietician to doctor, kit man to masseur, the film introduced us to some of the men in Sir Alex Ferguson's secret army, a special collection of men often known as the backroom boys. You might recognise some of the faces, but do you know their names? And what are their roles and responsibilities inside the Red machine? Read on...

Steve McClaren

He was perhaps the most famous face in Sir Alex Ferguson's support team for three seasons; in fact, some people thought he would be great as the next manager of United. As a player, Steve didn't exactly perform at the highest level (sorry, Hull, Oxford and co.) but as an **assistant manager**, he worked in the Premiership with Derby County before helping United win the Treble in his first half-season! He even coached the England national team for a few games during 2000/01.

One of his favourite training routines at Carrington was an exercise in which the lads had to sprint to either the left or the right, depending on his shout. At the same time, he would often point in completely the opposite direction, just to catch them out. The United players thought very highly of Steve and were sorry to see him leave for Middlesbrough in June 2001.

Jimmy Ryan

Unlike Steve, Jimmy did play at the highest level, for Manchester United! If you ever see a team photo from 1968, when the Reds first won the European Cup, you might spot him in the line-up. He was a tricky winger way back then, and he can still turn on the skill in training. Just ask Beckham, Butt, Giggs, Scholes and the Nevilles; Jim worked with them all during his time in charge of United Reserves from 1991 to 1999, and he's now training them again, as **first team coach**. In fact, while Fergie was away, he was even the manager for a day in December 1999. Unlucky for Jim, the Reds lost the match, 3–2 to Middlesbrough.

Tony Coton

TC also played for the Reds, but only in the Reserves while acting as cover for Peter Schmeichel in 1996. In fact, he was better known as a goalkeeper on the other side of town, with Manchester City. Before his spell with the Blues, he played for Watford and Birmingham City, where he saved a penalty on his debut. Now employed as United's specialist **goalkeeping coach**, Coton has helped Paul Rachubka and Nick Culkin to come through with confidence and make appearances in the first team.

Rob Swire

As **senior physiotherapist,** Rob's role is one of the most important at the club. It's his job on a match-day to keep his eye on the United players and be ready to rush on if any of them get injured. He has first-class first-aid skills and carries a well-stocked medical bag, which is designed to deal with on-the-pitch problems very quickly and cleanly. Rob is also a busy man during the week, helping his team of physios to prepare the club's many players for action by easing their aches, pains and strains. He might even be asked to test the fitness of a potential new signing, to make sure they're in the very best condition to play for United.

Dr Mike Stone

The job of football **club doctor** used to be part-time, but now that the medical side of the game is so important, and United have so many players, Dr Stone is now a full-time member of the backroom staff. Like his close colleague Rob Swire, the Doc is based in the medical centre at Carrington but travels with the first team wherever they go. He can prescribe medicines to the players if they're feeling ill, but he has to check carefully first, to make sure the tablets or drugs are not banned from use in professional football.

Albert Morgan and Alec Wylie

Ever wondered who has the nice job of washing the shirts, shorts and socks? Well, wonder no more, because Albert (pictured) and Alec are the **kit managers** who make sure the players are well turned out in red, white or blue. Helped by a team of laundry ladies, AM and AW are responsible for the collecting, cleaning, storing, transporting and sometimes the repairing of all the kit worn by all of the club's teams. Albert and Alec also have the keys to the special room where all the players' boots are kept.

Jimmy Curran and Trevor Lea

Jimmy (pictured) is part of the medical team at Carrington and Old Trafford. He's been at the club for more years than he'd like to admit to, serving with a smile and sometimes a song in various jobs, but most recently as **assistant to the physios** and **masseur** to the stars! Meanwhile, **club dietician** Trevor Lea makes sure the players consume the food and drink they need to perform at the highest level. Boiled rice, grilled chicken, fish and pasta may seem boring and bland compared to burgers and chips, but take it from Trev, they can do the trick!

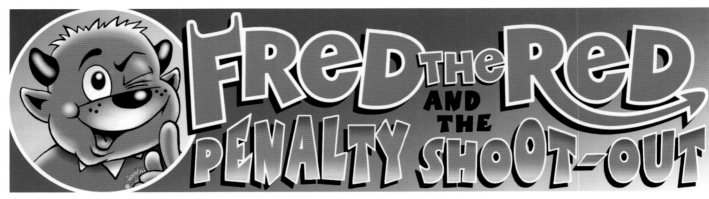

ANSWERS

Can You Win The Title?

1. Roy Keane
2. Phil Neville
3. Bradford City
4. Alan Hansen
5. Chief Executive
6. Goodison Park
7. ManUmobile
8. Chapman
9. Tony Coton
10. Ronny Johnsen
11. Keith Kent
12. Luke Chadwick
13. Roy Keane
14. Beyond The Promised Land
15. Van der Gouw and Yorke
16. Christian Karembeu
17. 1–0 to United
18. 5–1 to United
19. Teddy Sheringham
20. Valencia
21. Arsenal
22. Chelsea and Charlton
23. Ipswich Town
24. It was Hallowe'en
25. Germany
26. New Year's Eve
27. www.ManUtd.com
28. Dr Mike Stone
29. Southampton
30. Mr Halsey
31. Jimmy Floyd Hasselbaink
32. David Beckham and Gary Neville
33. Quinton Fortune
34. Ian Harte
35. Charlton and Coventry
36. Middlesbrough
37. White Hart Lane
38. 67 million guilders

Red Letters Quiz

A. Andrew Cole
B. Ronny Johnsen
C. Dwight Yorke
D. David Beckham
E. Ronnie Wallwork
F. Denis Irwin
G. Nicky Butt
H. Steve McClaren
I. Mikael Silvestre
J. Ryan Giggs
K. Ole Gunnar Solskjaer
L. Luke Chadwick
M. Roy Keane
N. Quinton Fortune
O. Ruud van Nistelrooy
P. Paul Scholes
Q. Sir Alex Ferguson
R. John O'Shea
S. Bojan Djordjic
T. Fabien Barthez
U. Gary Neville
V. Wes Brown
W. Michael Stewart
X. Raimond van der Gouw
Y. Phil Neville
Z. Jaap Stam